P9-CAY-024

did
u

know

When I was a
junior junior at
Pentagram in 1977,
Alan Fletcher used
to walk around his
team, and without
saying anything
help himself to one
of his assistant's
cigarettes, in front
of them. No one
said anything.
After a while of
this he came to my
desk again. As his
hand reached down
to my cigarettes,
I chirped up, *Either
pay me more money
so I can buy more
fags or F off and buy
your own.* A small
smile crossed his
mouth and ever
since then we've
got on very well
together.

What they didn't teach you in design school

Phil Cleaver

HOW
BOOKS

CINCINNATI, OHIO
WWW.HOWDESIGN.COM

I really enjoyed it, as I love your style of writing—it is exactly as you talk. What a great book.
Dorcas Guillebaud

16 15 14 13 12 5 4 3 2 1

ISBN 978–1–4403–3436–8

Designed and typeset by Worldwide Creative Head: Prof. Phil Cleaver Executive Visual Communicator: Emma Fisher, Translated into English by Rosanna Bianchini

For ILEX:
Publisher: Alastair Campbell
Executive Publisher: Roly Allen
Creative Director: James Hollywell
Managing Editor: Nick Jones
Commissioning Editor: Zara Larcombe
Art Director: Julie Weir
Color Origination:
Ivy Press Reprographics

Contents

> **Make lots of tea (even if you don't want one). It's a great way of getting to know colleagues and the perfect excuse to look over their shoulder and ask questions about what they do and what projects they are working on.**
> Julie Weir

This book is dedicated to
two people who have the
same initials: A.F.

Firstly to the designer
who let me open the magic
door of typography and
Pandora's box, and to
whom I owe so much,
Anthony Froshaug.

Also to the mighty
Alan Fletcher, who always
had time for everyone.
We made each other smile.
He gave me my first chance
to play in the game.

Dedicated to

it's
all about

Introduction

I give no rules,
as there are
no rules, and
if there were
I would only want
to break them.

Life after finishing college, and getting that all-important first foot on the ladder in the design industry, is no easy feat. Working in a studio is hugely different from studying; this book is aimed at helping you through the transition and giving you the ammo to climb this massive new learning curve.

With tens of thousands of design and advertising students graduating into the job market each year, it's more important now than ever before to be fully armed to succeed.

When I left art school, *graphic design* was the new description for commercial art and had not yet entered into the vocabulary of the general public. No one knew what graphic design was, and I even used to avoid telling people what I did, because I would then be forced to try to explain it—at that time it seemed too complicated. Now of course the application of graphics and graphic design is so widespread, in all its media, that it has become a household term.

Having been a maverick all my life, following my heart and not my head, I am in an odd position to be writing this book. I give no rules, as there are no rules, and if there were I would only want to break them.

However, what I do bring is the knowledge that comes with having been trained by some of the biggest and most influential names in graphic design. I've produced more than three decades' worth of award-winning work, run my own successful design agency, worked globally, and I now also teach as a professor in the creative industries.

Think of the world of professional design as a game, and you can't play the game if you are not yet in it. So, the first thing is to get yourself into the graphics game. This book guides you through the focal points and

useful

possible pitfalls at each and every stage of presenting yourself and your skills to the design industry.

Designers not only have to be able to design nowadays, they have to become project managers, sales people, client handlers, typesetters, art workers, and art directors. They need to write print specifications and control printers, not to mention be involved in prepress print production.

Graphic design now encompasses what used to be a lot of different professions; for example, it took an apprentice years to qualify as a compositer (typesetter) who could be trusted to set type. Now as a graphic designer, this is one of the skills you need to master. There is no graphic design without type, as it makes up 50 percent of most design work and it has to become a skill set, which to a designer is akin to breathing. The boundaries between professions are blurring as technology advances.

This book aims to guide you through the process from graduating to getting into a studio and staying there as a valued designer. It aims to be a useful guide and a bridge in the first year of your career.

Keep it with you; it will become an essential tool in your learning curve through your first year in the real world, it can be your companion and note book throughout the process, and hopefully it is your *get out of jail* card when you don't know where to turn.

ONE

GETTING
THROUGH
THE
DOOR

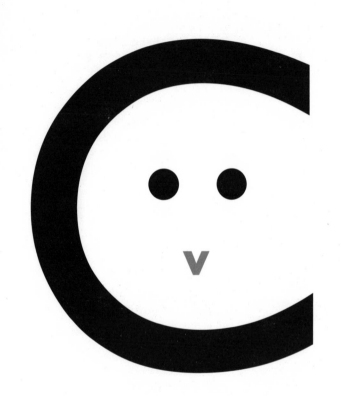

Your résumé

In the UK your résumé is called your CV, which is short for the Latin Curriculum Vitae.

We live in an increasingly open world. In today's society, with advancements made available globally by companies such as Google, you only have to type in a name and you can find people and contacts all over the world, whether it be on Facebook, LinkedIn, or other social media.

Given that you more often than not have your profile picture (or some sort of visual representation) on Facebook, it seems odd to me not to have an image on your résumé.

The point of a résumé is to help the prospective employer get to know you. It should not just be a list of educational achievements, but should somehow encapsulate as much information as possible about you and what you are like, all on one side of letter or A4 paper. Because it is a representation of you that is left behind after an interview, and read before your interview, your picture will help a prospective employer remember you.

You are seeking a job in a visual environment, so use a visual. It will not stop someone hiring you or offering you an interview; it is an advantageous aid to the recipient.

If you show you can't design and typeset your own résumé properly, an employer may think that you would apply this same poor treatment to any other design work entrusted to you.

The number of badly typeset and laid out résumés I have looked at is quite remarkable. Some could be classed as visual grievous bodly harm, they are so painful to look at.

A résumé should be treated as one of your major design jobs. The typeface you choose, the layout, etc.

all show exactly what level of design you are at. Every detail counts, and the sum of these details gives an impression of you as a designer.

Everything you do in the design world is a reflection of your design ability. Your résumé is a key part of the visual design campaign to get you noticed and remembered. Remember that you will be brought down to the level of your lowest piece of work.

If your portfolio looks great but your résumé is badly laid out and typeset, it will bring four years of learning and all of your hard work to date to nothing.

Your résumé needs to be viewed as an integral part of your visual armor and presentation to get you in the game.

Every résumé is different, but the most important thing is that a résumé should get across your personality when you are not physically present. Don't just typeset your résumé, design it as well and treat it as another design brief.

You should tailor your résumé to your specialty and reflect the content of your portfolio. A very elegant type solution will only work if that is what your portfolio looks like. It's all about trying to embed your passion, but never at the loss of clarity.

When putting your résumé together, include your best qualities, those that will give you an extra edge and make you stand out against your competition.

These qualities should be relevant to design and related skills that may be useful within the studio, such as English literature or another language, as such skills could come in handy when writing proposals, communicating with clients, or liaising with overseas clients, for example.

Even if you spent a year traveling around the world, turn your experience into a finished piece of design that shows you have the visual arts in your DNA.

It is very hard to stop a designer designing; it is a way of life, so show them you belong to that species.

Your résumé may be the thing that gets you an interview, but after the interview the prospective employer will probably sit with his short-listed candidates and then study their résumés. So make sure you design it well, to help prospective employers make the important decision to hire you and not the others.

If you have a good reference from somewhere you have worked previously or from an internship, then attach it to the back of your résumé. If you are currently still there, then ask them to write a reference even if they haven't paid you yet!

You can't play the game if you are not yet in the game.

reflɘction

You are in the
communication
business—
learn how to
communicate.

skills

Your portfolio

You must treat your portfolio as a design job, not just a collection of your best work. It has to be packaged like a product and clearly thought out. Great work will be diminished by a bad package.

The integral elements of your portfolio—the work itself, your typeset résumé, your online presence, and your calling card—should be presented as a cohesive package, a visually coordinated kit of parts.

You will already have the contents of the package: the best work from your design course. Take the kit of parts and package it up into a whole piece. Think of it like a book design, bearing in mind the order, pace, and flow of the contents.

Think of it as one of the most important design jobs you are ever going to do.

It is also important to work out what you show in each medium. I have interviewed people who turn up to the meeting with nothing, saying, *My portfolio is all online*. If you decide to only have an online portfolio and not spend time working on a printed version as well, you will have nothing to show and talk about in your interview.

A prospective employer is interested in seeing your physical skills in design as well as your software skills. For example, they will be looking to see if you can cut out straight or accurately, use spray adhesive, make up presentation boards, or put together mock-ups. This is communicated to and confirmed by them through looking at the actual work.

Design companies do not present their creative design concepts to clients by telling them to go look at something online, so this approach may not go down too well.

Analyze your target audience (the company you are presenting to) to work out what they like and go for it in their own visual language. They will respond to this.

You are in the communication business—learn how to communicate. If you can't learn how to communicate with your own industry sector, it's unlikely you can communicate a message to someone in any other sector, so why would a design firm hire you?

You have been trained for four years in how to think, solve visual problems, and communicate solutions. Your portfolio needs to go through the same process.

If you are thinking about including physical designs in your portfolio, like a piece of pack design or a magazine, then I believe that you can't beat putting in the real thing.

To be able to pick up a piece of packaging, examine it in your hands as you would if you were going to purchase it, is the best way for that design to be viewed.

The same goes with a brochure, magazine, or book. Your design should be looked at in the way you intended it to be seen and at the right distance from the eye. Any other way is one step removed from the original purpose.

There is only so much that you can carry around with you, so if you do bring physical products, make sure they are portable, and only bring the highest quality pieces that demonstrate your craft skills.

The problem with photographs of your work is that it is dependant on the level of your photography and the quality of the print that you make. Add the fact that this is all then put under a plastic sleeve in your portfolio, which also reduces the quality and impact of your design.

A designer, unlike a client, can read how good a design is from one visual. Seeing a design repeated in five different sizes and different color variations is not necessary and may not help the concept. It will also lose some visual impact and a lot of precious portfolio space.

However, the same design spread across a range of different deliverables is different as it proves the idea is flexible.

Also, try to have what I like to call a *hero* image, a wow image where they think, *Fuck, that looks good.*

You are seeking a job in a visual environment, so use a visual—this after all is your face to the design world.

Selecting your work

When selecting the projects that you are going to put into your portfolio, as a rough guide, I would suggest putting four or five really good pieces in, but if you have six or seven that are all of the same high standard, then show them all.

Balance is key. Just remember that the standard of your portfolio is brought down to the weakest piece, so if in doubt, leave it out.

Remember to rehearse what you have to say about each project. This way you'll not only have your spiel down pat, you'll also know how long it will take you. You should aim for about twenty minutes.

For the order of your portfolio, I would recommend putting the second-best piece of work up front, as the first job that your interviewer sees. This will get them interested and demonstrate that you know how to design for, communicate with, and guide an audience.

Put your strongest piece of work last, so you end on a high, and so that the project is a good talking point with which to continue the interview.

If you have done internships, and you are allowed to put the work you did in your portfolio, then I would keep it separate from the body of work you did at design school.

Internship work demonstrates what you can do in a professional studio, but you were probably part of a team, so when you talk about the work make sure you clearly explain what your input was and the amount of time you spent on it.

Your portfolio shows your talent, creativity, and how you solve design problems. It is about you, and this is what designers will evaluate in an interview.

If I'd had this book in my hand aged 21? I wouldn't have made a shambolic collection of mistakes and wrong turns. My career would have had structure, poise, and I would have said and done the right things at the right time (and probably done better work).
Michael Johnson

In my portfolio, I have never written anything to explain my work for the simple reason that I would never show my work without being there to talk through it, but in today's world this may not work.

At design school, you are taught to clearly explain the ideas, concepts, and outcomes of each design or project in notes and working sheets, so your process can be easily understood. This is because your work is looked at by a teacher without you being there. There has be a watertight guide to ensure you don't lose points because they didn't understand.

When showing your portfolio at an interview, this training will stand you in good stead, as you are now simply presenting it orally as opposed to writing it.

Some studios may ask you to drop your portfolio off. If so, use this situation as a way of developing an excuse to meet. For example, I would start the folder off with ten reasons why you wanted to meet them, along with a visual teaser; something that shows that you know how to design.

It is about your personality and your approach to creativity, and if those elements are the right fit then you can be trained in all the other parts you need to know and master.

about

What format?

The answer to what format your portfolio needs to be in will involve you looking at your work.

First of all, do not put your work into a large black art portfolio. It makes you look like you've just left art school and you don't know how to package your work professionally.

Approach your portfolio presentation just like you would the presentation of any other visual idea. For example, if you want to design for screen-based work then you need to present your work on a computer, as that's the format it should be viewed on.

Alternatively, if you want to be a magazine designer, then turn your portfolio into a magazine in which your work becomes the magazine's content. These are all ways to start to speak to designers in their own visual language.

Keep the format relevant and congruent with your work but at the same time ensure that, whichever format you decide it to take, it is practical and portable. It will make your life a lot easier when it comes down to it.

I once interviewed a very well-dressed, petite designer whose portfolio was gigantic, and she could hardly lift it. I even had to help her lift it onto the table. ! wondered how she had got her portfolio to the studio, let alone carry it around town. As I suspected, when I opened her portfolio there was only one poster that needed the size, while the rest of the work was like her, petite in format. I told her, for the next time we meet, to get a portfolio to fit her! I explained that her portfolio is an extension of her, to think of it as a fashion accessory. She is petite, so her portfolio then also needs to be petite and delightful.

If you have one large poster, simply put it in a roll and then unroll it during the interview. This way the size will be an advantage, because it shows you can work big, as well as providing some showmanship as you unroll it.

You will be carrying your work all over the place when doing rounds of interviews, so make it something that is easy for you to manage and that works to your advantage.

You do not want too many pieces of work on show at the same time. If you were to present four magazine spreads simultaneously, your eyes wouldn't know which way to look as each spread fights for attention. Show the spread as it is meant to be viewed: in an actual magazine, held in your hand, one spread at a time. After all, that's how you designed it to work, not stuck down flat next to other pages under a plastic sleeve.

The same goes for book designs. The potential viewer needs to see it, touch it, and hold it in their hands just like they would if it was the final outcome. So design the format of your portfolio the way you designed the contents to be viewed. If you end up with a small pile of objects, such as magazines and books, these can be packaged in a clamshell box or in a photographer's presentation case. The presentation of your work says a lot about you.

One of the best portfolios I have viewed lately was designed into the format of a book. This young designer had designed the whole package, and her book portfolio came in a cloth slipcase. The book was well crafted and well designed. The production was also great, which supported the well-designed work in the book. The whole package was well thought out. Not only was her work put into this unique format, but the work inside was also displayed suitably.

Get a sense of how designers look at other designers' work, study design magazines and design annuals—there are plenty of them! This can help you develop suitable ways to produce your portfolio format.

Whichever way you package your folder, it is going to take a while to get it perfect. It's always a good idea to include something you have made or mocked up, as hand skills are still important in a studio. I can tell a lot about a designer from the way something is put together, such as skill with a scalpel, attention to detail, and visual awareness of space.

As an employer, I would want your help to mock designs up to take to clients, so the way you treat your own work will be a reflection of how you are going to treat the design projects in my studio.

pack*age*

PDF portfolios

When contacting studios for work, sometimes they will ask you to send over your portfolio. The design company uses this as the quickest way of sorting out who is worth meeting.

So in this case you have to take your kit of parts—your portfolio and your content—and design a specific PDF just to get through this selection process. Even if you end up with an iconic photograph of a really good, mouth-watering shot of a cup of coffee and the words *I make a good cup of coffee,* it's still using your skill set to stand out.

A portfolio of work is something that you show and as such it needs to be presented by you, in person. If you are putting up work to be judged online, it should be presented differently from your portfolio; it will need some text to take the viewer through your design process, but try to keep this to a minimum otherwise it will distract the eye from your work.

If and when a studio or designer does ask for you to send over your portfolio in PDF version, treat it like a website and make it more of a teaser than a full display of your work. Entice them to call you in to see your full portfolio.

If you don't get selected after giving your best shot, don't worry. You may not have been right for that particular design firm. It's a little like dating: there are a lot more fish in the sea, you just have to find the right one. In the end it will work out, so persevere.

You can always e-mail back the person who said no thank you (if they had the manners to do that) and ask them for feedback. It may help you get through next time. Don't forget, it's only one person's opinion of your work, and someone else might feel differently.

How to get through the door

individual

To get into the game, the first hurdle is to find the door. To open any door you have to find the handle.

It's no different when trying to get through the door of a design company to present your work; you have to find the handle, a handle on which to hang your approach. It also means you will need different approaches to the various areas of the design industry—you can't expect an advertising agency to respond in the same way as a design company, as the people working in each field are normally very different.

The competition for places is high, and you will have to stand out from the crowd. However, you already have the key: you are an individual and you design differently from your friends at university.

As in life, everyone is unique—your personality, your approach to life, your feeling of self-worth, your confidence, your likes and dislikes.

As you look at the work in your degree show, you will see the difference between your work and that of your fellow students. Likewise, you can also see the diversity in each of your friends' work.

What you must do is recognize, explore, and expand on your own unique qualities. What makes you tick, design-wise, and what makes you different from others? This quality can be developed into something that stands out. You have got the core essence of this in your work, and your portfolio, so study it, get to know and appreciate it.

Contacting the agency by e-mail or letter is a crucial initial form of communication. If you write a standard letter and e-mail it or post it out en masse, not having bothered to find out the recipients' names, whoever reads it in the design company will be able to tell you have just sent out a mass mailer, with no personal consideration of them. So why should they consider you?

The response rate to even the best written and designed mailers is probably less then one percent in this game. You literally want and need to find a way to kick down the door, not just politely and quietly knock on it, hoping that someone might hear. Finding that personal contact is a great start.

Even the way you knock on that door will convey something about you, so think about your approach beforehand.

The formula is really quite straightforward, it just needs care and attention to detail. Initially you need to look at your work and analyze the essence. Work out how to project your strongest visual piece. Then think about where you want to work and to which sort of company you would be suited. Are you going to work at the biggest company or for a small design firm? You should get to know the design group and what makes them tick, as well as researching the most relevant contacts there and making a note of their names and positions.

All of these points should help you see who you truly are and find your passion in what you do. Getting your foot through that door is the first big step into a design group. Like any design problem, use those newly learned skills you have spent the last few years developing and paying for, and then apply them to this next major project.

language

E-mailing studios

Using e-mails as a method of making first contact with studios is a waste of time, especially if you haven't done your research thoroughly to find the correct e-mail address or the appropriate person to send it to. If your message ends up in the wrong place, it just shows that you haven't bothered and your e-mail will get trashed.

Having said that, e-mails work better if you are into digital design and your work is only ever meant to be seen on screen.

I would send the designer something tangible to get them interested; you can then follow this up with an e-mail. Even the best e-mails from graduates normally get overlooked or thrown out. You can't afford to take this chance.

The worst e-mails are those that start *To whom it may concern, please go to this link and look at my work.* As a professional, why would I bother taking the time to look at someone's work if the person e-mailing me hasn't bothered to put more effort in?

It reflects poorly on you if you don't care about your work, how you present it, and how it is viewed. The recipient will be inclined not to care either.

On the other hand, if I were to receive a beautifully produced and crafted piece of communication, which I can hold in my hands, it would trigger all the right emotions, because the sender would be speaking to me in my language.

The language of design triggers the heart and then the mind.

The importance of being proactive

> There's more to being a designer than having a computer; you have to show your creative skills and add value to everything you work on no matter how small the job.
> Jo Allnutt

presented

Following the steps you have learned over the last four years, you need to tackle the job of getting through the door of your chosen design firm just as you would any other design job or brief (using research, analysis, and problem-solving). Once you have worked out what the actual problem is, you need to begin to solve it in the same manner.

If you tackle this as a design brief in your own way, it stops it becoming a bore and the answer will come. To get results, you have to put the effort in; you only get back what you put in.

It is important to research all prospective design firms. They will each have a website, so study their work. Does your work look like it would fit in?

This research will give you the information you need to compose your introduction, so take care to make notes on the work of each design company. Write down what impressed you about their work and include some of this information in your approach; everyone likes positive comments about their work. It shows you have done your homework and that you're inspired enough to want to be a part of their team.

The hardest part of your job search is getting that first interview, so put the bulk of your time and effort into that goal. It's also important to make sure that you stay in touch afterward. Don't let all your hard work go to waste.

The person you met and presented to in the studio now knows you and your work, which will make keeping in touch afterward a lot easier. Find your own way and use it to keep that relationship alive.

Any technical skill can be learnt, any process mastered, any computer tamed. Likewise you can adapt, modify, plagiarize, bastardise as much as you like. But none of the above will produce true creativity.

True creativity comes from you. Pure you. And no university, internship, boss or computer can teach you that. That is your choice, your responsibility.

Commit to you and you will truly create.

Otto Bathurst

Ways to open the door

> There's a lot of
> awful design out
> there.
> If you can tell the
> difference you're
> halfway there.
> If you can make
> a difference,
> you've arrived.
> Phil Clements

Kicking open the doors into the design industry will require a few fundamental tools that can be adapted to the appropriate sector.

The letter, the e-mail, the mailer, and your website are all you need in your gym bag to truly play in this game. Most students, quite rightly, spend all their time and effort putting their utmost into producing the final year show, but it's not until the last minute that they realize they need a business card to hand out at the show. So they put one together quickly and haphazardly, and that's where the problem lies.

Designing a card and letterhead at the last minute is not the correct approach if you want to impress the world with your design skills. Your own visual identity needs as much careful consideration, analysis, research, development, and polish as the rest of the work in your portfolio does.

If you can't create it easily, don't worry (many design companies have not solved this problem), just design a very simple, well-crafted bit of type. You'll need at least this for a letter or an e-mail.

I still think a well-composed letter on a good letterhead with nice-quality paper, eloquently written with no spelling mistakes, says more about you than the same content in an e-mail. To this day, I absolutely love getting mail to open.

Never forget that the layout of the letter is just as important as the words you write. You are in the visual game after all. In addition, I think the visual effect of a letter works for all of the industry because it shows more care and attention than any e-mail. You can always follow up a letter with an e-mail, but first impressions count for a lot. The material of your letterhead is a good way of showing your approach

33

to design. A letter is a three-dimensional object, and the attention to detail will convey a lot about you to potential employers.

I have received some very nice pieces of design through the post over the years from various designers. One particular piece that stood out was from an Australian designer whose last name was Berry.

It came as a four-page leaflet and had been beautifully designed, all based around fruit berry tea with tea bags attached. It was a good visual pun on her name. The last line of text said, *I also make a good cup of tea.* I hired her, and she was a brilliant assistant for three years, before moving back down under, and she did make rather good tea.

Your website only wants to be a teaser to get someone interested in you and your work.

Your website is the final tool, but if you put all your best pieces on your website you'll have nothing new to wow them with in the interview.

You have to make an impression against your competition and if you give it all away upfront you will lose this *wow* factor, so be careful about what you present digitally.

teaser

2

TWO

INTERVIEWS

show

What to take and show

Having analyzed your target design firm, go back and refresh your knowledge on the company by studying their website again. Don't just take note of their visual portfolio, but take in how they talk and write about themselves, their work, and their client list. A client list may contain a large proportion of past clients, but this does show their pedigree and history.

Your portfolio is a collection of parts made up from different components you have designed during your time at design school. Use these pieces to tailor your portfolio toward the design firm you are going to see, selecting the work that would fit into their way of designing.

If you have one piece of design that fits well, see if you can design more pieces to expand the project to the same high standard.

Your portfolio is not about quantity, it's about quality. It's better to have four brilliant pieces of work than have ten pieces of work to show, especially if the other six pieces reduce the impression of the better four. Careful selection shows an understanding of the target firm's market sector as well as expertise in their requirements; it also offers some common ground on which to build a bond. Use your design experience, and sector knowledge to get through their shields.

I have seen far too many pages of design students' portfolios where they want to show you their ability to use certain media by inserting a few examples that bear no relationship to their design work.

You are being hired as a designer primarily, not for you to draw or to take photos. If the design firm wants this, then they can hire a top photographer in the relevant field. It does however show me that you have skills, which you could put to use if and when the need arises, and it may give you an edge over your competition.

I therefore think it's a good idea to show this skill set by starting to develop it. If you're aiming to entice a graphic design company that does a lot of print work, make your drawing, photo, or Illustrator piece into a work of graphic design.

For example, put your photo or illustration on a book cover, turn it into a poster or incorporate it into some packaging. It shows your idea being used in the context of design. However, always be prepared to consider this application a little more deeply. Design the jacket using the totality of your piece, considering the work as the solution to a problem, thereby giving it relevance from start to finish.

That then gives you a piece of graphic design, and you can also explain how you solved the brief. That's called post-rationalization.

Problem-solving has to be the main strength of a designer, as that's what you're getting hired to do: solve a client's set of communication objectives by using graphics to get the message across.

The graphics, in most cases, will speak for themselves; however, never underestimate the importance of your own verbal communication skills with your client/ future employer.

You're selling yourself, so you need to have a product to pitch. Show how good your solutions are to visual problems.

The key is to believe in yourself, because if you don't, no one else will.

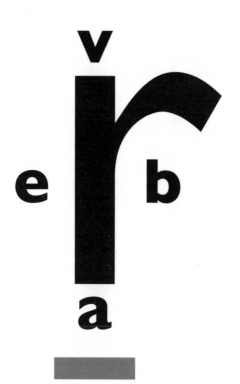

Way back in 1975, when I was a graphics student at Ravensbourne College of Design and Communication, I did a month's professional practise as Alan Fletcher's assistant at Pentagram. I remember that white-knuckle adventure like it was yesterday. It was bloody hard work. There was never enough time and always too much to get done. And they kept the studio tidy. Blimey, that was a shock. I've a vivid memory of my portfolio assessment. It was Plymouth Boy meets Father of British Graphic Design. It was a bruising encounter with reality. You're just pissing about, he said.

The thing that sticks in my mind most about my time at Pentagram is realizing how little I actually knew—rather than how much I thought I knew—and how much I had to learn if I was going to live by my ideas. Everything I'd learned at Ravensbourne was put in perspective. And like all graphics students, up till then I really had no idea what being a professional designer was all about.

Most of the things I got to do were anything but glamorous. It was dogsbody work, as you'd expect. But it taught me that in this business, attention to detail is everything. So when you're first starting out, tolerate the dull stuff and focus instead on grabbing every opportunity to pick as many brains as you can.

Helping put together presentations taught me how to sell ideas. I'd always imagined that good ideas sell themselves. They don't. The best ideas are the hardest to sell. The better your ideas, the harder you're going to have to ram them down people's throats. When I look back on those early years that's one of the most valuable lessons I learned.

I was asked back a few times after I left Ravensbourne, so the Father of British Graphic Design couldn't have thought I was too bad. Or maybe I just got better.

John Spencer

Know the design company's work

The more visual knowledge of a company's design work you have, the better. In college you were trained to research, so don't let this skill go to waste. Find out as much as you can and start to compile your information so you are prepared.

You have learned to research any design job before starting to inform yourself about the competition and to help you get to know what you are dealing with before you can accumulate your design ideas. This is no different. Design companies are all competing with each other for work, which should make your task considerably easier.

Their website has been painstakingly designed to communicate who they are, to showcase their work and demonstrate to potential clients why their work is better than any other design company. Their sites will also normally have background information on the principles of that company. Look at their profile and work out if this sort of work is what you aspire to do.

Would you love to have design jobs like theirs under your belt and in your portfolio?

The more you know a company's work, the easier it is to develop a dialogue with them. If you have something to talk to them about, it is a good selling point in this game.

Being interested in their work makes you interesting to them, but beware that bullshit won't work, so you have to stay true to what you believe in.

The first job you get can be very important as it is the stepping-stone to your next job. As you progress in your career, your portfolio will gradually change. Your college work will get replaced with the work you have done professionally in design companies.

Our future depends on people like you, who see the world differently. So use your creative brain; it's an unparalleled tool.
Jim Thompson

You can get pigeonholed in this game very fast. Everyone wants to put you in a named box.

In design, you're a packaging designer, a print designer, or a web designer. In advertising, you are an art director, copywriter, typo, or finished art.

Once you are tagged, it is normally quite hard to get untagged. If you spend even a year doing nothing but packaging, your portfolio quickly becomes more concentrated in that area and before you know it you have the portfolio of a packaging designer. It then becomes very hard to branch out into a branding company.

Twenty-nine years ago, I interviewed a very talented young designer who had spent the beginning of his career in publishing designing some great book covers, but Lee Comber wanted to get into a more mainstream design company. He was caught in a catch-22 because his portfolio was only full of book covers, so he was only being offered jobs doing exactly that. I could see his potential and offered him a job. The rest is design history.

I believe that great designers are great designers whatever they design, but the world loves labels. My solution is to wear different hats and make sure that I am able to work across any design discipline. It is important to be multi-disciplinary to get the variety of problem-solving design briefs I enjoy.

know

polish up

What to wear

An interview is similar to a first meeting, going on a date, or meeting your partner's parents for the first time. What you wear and how you wear it communicates a lot about you to the person or people interviewing you.

I think you need to look like you have made some degree of effort and aim to look your best. Look smart, think smart. You have designed all your portfolio elements up to this point to look their best. This is the last bit in that journey of communication. You have polished up your work; now polish up yourself.

It is important to be yourself and to wear what makes you feel good. Remember, you are out to impress. Being your natural self is important.

I used to dress in Edwardian frock coats, pinstriped trousers, dress vests, shirts with detachable collars, and always wore a tie…but then again I have always been a bit strange to say the least. Alan Fletcher used to ask me when I was going to stop wearing my late grandfather's clothes.

Being immaculately dressed in black and white with just a touch of red reflected my typographical work. You do not want to dress up to the extent that your clothes draw the attention away from your portfolio. I have hired punks with pink spiky hair, long-haired hippies, new romantics, and people with piercings all over their faces. Normally, colorful people have colorful portfolios, and what counts in this game is your portfolio.

While at college, the whole focus, correctly, is on what grade you get for your degree. But once you leave, no one is bothered about what grade you got; they are only interested in your portfolio and your

talent as a designer, and subsequently, what you can
do as a designer for their business. But if you got the
highest grade, there is no harm in making sure you
communicate this, because it is an endorsement of
your skill set.

Don't forget that apart from assessing your work,
your prospective employer is thinking about whether
you will fit into their studio and get on with their staff.

Allow your personality to come out in the interview,
because they also have to work out what you will be
like under pressure, sometimes working very late at
night with the rest of their designer gang.

horror stories

*For a top job interview you will have to show some brilliant
work. But it will also be important to communicate that
you are resourceful, can go the extra mile, and have the
ability to deliver under pressure.*

*When I interviewed designers and I liked what they were
producing, I would then ask them, What was the worst
moment so far?*

*Some told horror stories of very expensive photo shoots;
others, the wrong client presentation in the bag. What
this did for me was to gain an insight into how they
behaved when things went wrong and they were put
under pressure. Also, what they learned and took away
from these nasty experiences.*

If any of the things below fit, you should be OK.

• I had a better idea so re-did the project overnight.
*• I didn't like the first results, so I did a re-shoot at
  the weekend.*
• A tough problem needed a lot of research in the bar.

Be lucky,
John Larkin

Interview preparation

The priorities I outline here are things I do naturally and have been doing for over thirty years. I always get to where my interview appointment is 30–40 minutes ahead of time. I never rush.

Once I have got to their front door (which ensures I know exactly where I have to be at the allotted time), I turn around and walk off to do whatever, get a drink, sit on a bench. I can relax, because I know I am going to be on time. I open up my computer and get my work loaded up ready to present, so all I'll have to do is open the lid.

I have sat in interviews watching people scrambling to just start their computers, never mind launch programs, find the file, etc. Sadly, it just proves you haven't done your preparation.

You don't want to waste any of the time in an interview; you are selling yourself and creating that all-important first impression. Be prepared: it reflects what you will be like to work with.

Rehearse what you are going to say about each piece of work you show—if you can't summarize your own work down to a few key sentences, it demonstrates you're not going to deal with complicated concepts very well. Distill the brief/problem and your solution.

Bob Gill used to say that if you can't sell the idea over the phone you haven't got a clear proposition.

I did a retail brand whose brief was, We want something that says we are British and proud, but with street cred. I gave them a British bulldog wearing sunglasses. When I presented it, the big boss's first words after seeing the symbol were, Are you taking the piss, sonny? The directors who had hired me began to walk out of the meeting (but I still sold it in).

45

communicate

If you write down the brief/solution for each piece of work, it will help you to be more precise when describing it in the interview. You have to be able to sell your work, and if you can't show you believe in it, you're not going to succeed.

One of the best tests for a successful idea is how simply and quickly it can be communicated. If you talk too long about what the idea is, you know it doesn't really work. The work must speak for itself; you are the voiceover while the work is center stage.

You will communicate your passion for design by the way you talk about your design work, so just be yourself and don't worry, because the person interviewing you isn't worried either—they just want to see what you can offer.

Only show your best pieces, even if you don't have many. At least you know you are showing what is strong. It also demonstrates your design judgment, that you know what is good and what isn't, and that you have a discerning eye and you are not afraid to edit your design.

If you had a great idea from the first or second year, it is probably still a great idea, so redesign it purely so it looks great in your portfolio.

A designer should always be able to make and break the grid!
Sibyl Cherry Lai

The interview

Try to remember which way you came in.
Don't try to exit through the closet! Done that.
Steve Twigger

From the minute you walk into the interview room, you are beginning to give an impression of yourself, including your body language, where you look, and even how you sit down. For God's sake smile—this is not the dentist, and you should look like you want to present your work.

You might produce great, creative work but you have to fit into an agency; they are looking for someone who will dovetail into their already well-oiled studio.

The work should sell itself, so you have to sell yourself. Be true to yourself; you have packaged yourself the way you are, now it's time to unwrap that package and shine.

Make sure you have studied their work to see if anything you have is a similar style. If your work gels with them, you can bring the conversation around to their work and speak passionately about it.

Always offer to intern for a few weeks, which gives them the opportunity to try before they buy. Your enthusiasm to get in that studio should be infectious.

What you say, how you act, how you bring out your portfolio or laptop, how you place them on the table, and whether you make eye contact are all as important as your work itself.

I use a sixth sense more than most; through my dyslexia and lack of understanding from the spoken word I read people very quickly. I have hired people without looking at their work, because by talking to them I know if they have the potential to design well or not.

Don't forget to mention any additional skill sets apart from design if you have them. For example, if you have

interview

the highest grade in English it can be an extra selling point as most designers can't write or proofread well.

If you have lived or traveled abroad, survived doing any work, etc., it shows initiative and an ability to cope in different situations. Always get across the fact that you're willing to go that extra mile to get the job you want.

Always thank people. Ask for feedback about your work and interview technique, as any pointers they can give you about any of it will be useful. If you don't agree afterward, go ahead and dismiss them, unless you keep hearing the same comment. Do something about it.

If they were encouraging about your work, ask for their contacts; you could use their name to go to see another designer.

Having got your foot through the door, stay in touch: send an example of another design job, even something you found. It is hard enough to get your foot in the door, so once you have stay in touch.

Most of the time I see a designer once and never hear from them again. People like working with people they know, so use your heart and mind to connect with them.

**It's your enthusiasm,
intelligence,
creativity, diligence,
and mindfulness that
people want from
you. Hone these
skills constantly.**
Keren House

do your homework

For a Creative Director in the mid-eighties, it was hard to find talented designers who could do (or begin to learn) visual identity at the level we needed. I had doubled the number of our designers up to thirty-five in eighteen months, which meant we were constantly interviewing designers. Finding the brilliant designers out there is never easy (while managing them is another story altogether). My adage is to always hire people who have the potential to be better than you.

The funniest interview I did was jointly with Werner, a brilliant Swiss designer who had a lovely dry sense of humor. I was a bit late for the start of the interview, and as I came into the room, I told Werner to keep going and I sat down. At this point I had been responsible for most of the printwork on 3i, one of my claims to fame while in my previous job at Wolff Olins, and had designed all the Insight and Guide series.

The interviewee turned over the page of his portfolio and started to show Werner and me covers and spreads from the 3i Insight and Guide series. Before Werner could say anything, I started to ask some pertinent questions about this work that the designer of a job should be able to answer, for example, why had he used this particular typeface? I wanted to see how good a bluffer this guy was. If he could have pulled it off, and told a convincing story, I might well have hired him nonetheless; anyone who had the effrontery to pull that off showed he could sell graphics, and that's half the battle. But he hadn't done his homework, and his answers to my probing questions weren't convincing. I was starting to have fun.

Eventually Werner thought he should put this designer out of his misery and asked him, Do you know who he is? He looked at me and said, No, sorry, we weren't introduced. Werner said, That's Phil Cleaver. The guy just stood up, closed his portfolio, didn't say a word, turned around, and walked straight out of the room. I was on the floor laughing.

> **If you don't ask the question, you will never know what the answer is.**
> Karen Billingham

Ask the interviewer questions

If your interview is going well and they seem to like you and your work, but they tell you they can't employ you or give you an internship because they are full right now, you can use this line: *I have my own laptop with my own programs on it, surely if you're busy you can use a spare pair of hands, I'll only need a corner of the desk and it's not costing you anything.* See how they get out of that one.

If that's not an option, always find when you could intern. If you get offered a place or an internship you should still ask questions: hours of work, what will you be doing, how long is your trial period…anything you are unsure about.

If you're interning always ask if there is any chance of petty cash. No harm in asking; you can only get told no.

If this is still not going anywhere, ask if they know someone else in another studio who would see you and your work. You can use their name to open that door. I get called by some other designers asking me if I would look at someone's work because it's very good. I also get letters (which I prefer) saying so-and-so says I should get in touch to show you my portfolio. In both cases I always see them. Word of mouth and the contact system works.

don't sell

Six months after graduating from college and a long struggle of trying to find a full-time position, I was invited to an interview with a small, commercial art gallery in London. The position I had applied for was pretty much my perfect job. I was really excited; the interview went well and the next day (a Friday) they offered me the job, starting on Monday.

I was ecstatic. I quit my part-time job and my internship, I went shopping for new clothes suitable for work in a

> **Design is performance art, not for the fainthearted, to be practiced and performed everyday, regardless—executed with a passion and enjoyment of doing and learning consistently.**
> Richard Ward

gallery. On Saturday I received my contract, which I read through carefully with my parents. There were parts about the contract I really wasn't happy about; there was a clause stating I could do no freelance work or work with anyone who had anything to do with the gallery including its clients, customers, suppliers, and staff, both while I was working for them and if I left the job for a year afterward.

This annoyed me slightly. The design industry is supposed to be creative—I understand they didn't want me to steal their clients, but most designers do freelance work on the side of their main job. Alongside this there was no detail about career progression, and the salary specified was much lower than the figure advertised—so low that by the time I had commuted to and from work I would have less than one hour's minimum wage a week to live on!

My parents persuaded me the best thing to do was to ring my employer to discuss the contract. I politely asked whether there were any salary reviews, for which my employer (for want of a better description) went crazy over the phone at me. He said I was lucky he had offered me the job and that I should be grateful. He also told me any sensible graduate out of college would have been happy with the salary he was offering me, and the fact I asked for an increase made me greedy and led him to question whether I was the right person for the job, at which point he withdrew my job offer and hung up!

I learned that I probably had a lucky escape. You don't have to work for businesses that aren't going to appreciate and value you as an employee. You have every right to question your contract, especially when it comes to money.

I felt unmotivated and unhappy for a long time at having to begin looking for a job again, but everything happens for a reason. You have to pick yourself up and believe in the talent you have—don't sell yourself short!

Hannah Catchlove

cell phones

The weirdest interview I ever had came a few years after college. A designer whom I'd respected for a long time invited me to interview with him. Naturally, I was excited.

I bought a ticket with my own money and flew four states away to meet him. I sat in his lobby. He'll be right with you. *Two hours later, I still had not met him. I remember wishing I'd brought a book. Around hour three, the receptionist asked for my cell phone number. My cell rang.* Leland, I'm so sorry. I'm in Chicago and won't be able to meet you. *I was annoyed, but my Southern manners came through.* It's OK. I'm happy to reschedule.

A month later, we set a new meeting time. I emptied a little more of my bank account. This time it was for lunch. My cell rang. Leland, I'm so sorry. I'm in Los Angeles and won't be able to meet you. It's OK, I'm happy to reschedule. *I wasn't. How could he possibly do this again? But I still wanted to work with him. A new date set. Another bank debit.*

More crappy airline peanuts. This time we picked breakfast. I told the waiter I'd prefer to order when my guest arrive. Two hours later, I enjoyed my breakfast alone. I was starving and uninterested in rescheduling, ever. Halfway through my oatmeal, he arrived. Good morning Leland, how are you? *I would have loved to have heard that salutation three months earlier. The conversation was great. Lester Beall. Branding. Computer hacking. Joseph Campbell. Bauhaus. An hour later, he hired me. At the table.*

Years later, he was set to interview a new design candidate who patiently waited in the lobby. I reminded him of this and to not be late. But I like to be late, *he quipped. Baffled, I inquired why.* Because how they respond tells me a lot about them. *He smiled. I laughed.* So, *he added,* what's his cell number?

Leland Maschmeyer

> **Designers see the world in a different way. The trick is in the communication.**
> Nikki Wollheim

How to be remembered

If you have followed the tips throughout this book, then you should have a thorough and well worked-out portfolio, and you will have impressed the designer who interviewed you.

By presenting your visual brilliance and graphic dexterity alongside your problem-solving abilities, you should be well remembered for your work.

I would certainly advise you to always have something to leave behind, maybe a non-creased résumé, an extended résumé, or an actual example of your best piece of work.

Business cards can also be a helpful reminder to the interviewer. But the design of that card has to be as good as anything in your portfolio. It is a representation of yourself and one that deserves a great design.

You must look at your interviews in a similar way to any new business activity. The hardest part is getting that first meeting.

Afterwards, you must find a way of keeping in touch; it shows you're on the ball. It will keep you at the front of their minds.

This is important because if he/she needs a junior designer you'll be recalled. Also, if someone else asks them if they have seen any good talent, they can say that they know a really good young designer who is communicative and attentive.

The person in the studio who interviewed you now knows you and your work, and has a great résumé or your card at hand. By finding some way of staying in touch with them, you'll be able to occasionally update them.

You should have their personal e-mail, so send them some more work, recent stuff, showing you are still designing even if you're not employed yet.

Always keep a good record of your interviews and who you've met or spoken to, because you never know when you'll need to refer to it.

Build your own database of people you have been interviewed by; anything you do to stand out from the crowd will help!

sell yourself

be cheeky

*At my degree show, this distinguished older gentleman
asked me to come and show my work at his studio. As
he walked off, I called after him, I would if I knew your
name. He replied, I'm Henrion and I'm in the book
[telephone book]. This was FHK Henrion, who ran one of
the first studios specializing in corporate identity; one of
the first great gods of graphics. After the show I rang his
studio, explained the exchange, and I was asked to show
my portfolio and given a time to visit. I was impressed; it
was in the countryside, Hampstead, in Pond Street where
he had converted part of his house into a very beautiful
modern design studio. I met his two senior designers,
Chris Ludlow and Klaus Schmidt. I started the interview by
asking them to show me the work of the Henrion Studio
(there was no internet then), and afterwards I showed
mine. In the back of my head I was thinking, I don't
want to do this sort of work, it's boring.[†] Ludlow and
Schmidt seemed very entertained by my portfolio, which
consisted of only type and books. The whole process
took about an hour, and by the end we mutually agreed
this was not the right place for me to start my career,
but instead could I please go through my portfolio again,
showing the rest of the designers in the studio my work.
I duly did. I saw neither hide nor hair of the great man
Henrion himself.*

Once I got home, I wrote Henrion an invoice, For
entertaining your studio for one hour, the fee of
£10.00, *and smiled as I posted it to him. I never got paid!
But from then on, while phoning up for more interviews
elsewhere, I was told I could come and show my work, but
they didn't want an invoice. It was this prank that got me
through a lot of doors.*

[†]*Out of my thirty-five years in the design industry,
I have spent the better part of thirty of them producing
nothing but corporate identities, such as re-branding
VISA worldwide. To date I have designed over 130 visual
identities, despite me believing when I went for that
interview what they did was not for me!*

FAIR

trade

Internship

You can't get a job because you have no experience, and you can't get experience if you can't get a job. This old chicken and egg situation has been going on from time immemorial.

I think that the more internships you have done while at college the better. Some courses allow for a year in the industry before their third year.

This is a great idea as you learn skills on your internship and how the design industry works—you can see the difficulties in getting great creative work through clients. You then take all your developed skills back into college and use them to design your final degree show.

It will help you realize that your final year is the only time that you can design whatever you want and the way you want, without interference from a client. It is a unique time to show your talents which you may not get ever again, or until much later in your career.

After completing University, an internship is that vital experience you need to get in the game. It also lets a prospective design company try you out. You both get to see what the other is like before there is any commitment to a full-time job.

If you really want to work somewhere, it is a good idea to offer that you are willing to do an internship to prove your worth to them and show how you can fit into their company and become an irreplaceable part of it.

Getting to try the goods before you buy is a great proposition. It is up to you to prove your worth, but it also gives you the chance to discover whether you like them or working there. It is way out without anyone losing face.

An internship has to be symbolic; make sure you and the design company get something from it. You want to get a piece of professionally designed work for your portfolio, and they are getting a free design. That way it is a fair trade. If all you get is the work that other designers in the studio don't want to do, that isn't a fair trade.

You are getting nothing for your portfolio that will demonstrate your developing experience. If this is the case then you should take it to the boss.

You are not going to get far sitting on your ass taking all the crap. Explain to the boss that you don't mind doing that sort of work and starting from the bottom when you are getting paid for it, but it's not a fair trade if you have nothing to show at the end of your internship.

During your internship, make the coffee and tea before being asked. Try to fit in and find ways for people to notice that you are interactive. Always offer to stay late, join in, and become part of that design family.

Make yourself irreplaceable. Do this and you stand a better chance of them offering you a job.

There is a thin line, though; do not become a puppy, always being too helpful and crawling up to people. This will not get you very far, and you will become a nuisance more than a help, always seeking attention.

The firing incident

Between my second and third year of college I took a six-month graphic design placement in a non-design related business. This proved to be a pretty good benchmark and a great learning experience for me for a number of reasons. I was very green in terms of design.

My skills in creative suite were limited. I had only had two years at college doing graphic design without any previous experience in the field as I had a more traditional art-related (painting and drawing) background. This meant I failed… a lot. I found it difficult to produce things quickly and to visualize my ideas. The placement was also more on the corporate side of things. Designs often needed to be refined and polished, something I really wasn't great at, especially under pressure with someone looking over my shoulder.

After six months of struggling, being unhappy and feeling constantly down about my skills, creativity, and prospects in the industry, I was let go. Although it didn't feel like it at the time, this was probably the best thing that could have happened to me. It made me realize that this side of design was only one part of the industry, and, frankly, one that didn't inspire me too much at that time. This pushed me to try my hand at illustration as well as other projects that grabbed me. I took another placement afterwards that proved much more fruitful, and I learned more in the next six months than the first two years of college. It propelled me into my final year with renewed drive, a sense of purpose, and active interest in the industry. The main thing I learned—though this is Brie-level cheesy but important nonetheless so bear with me—it taught me to trust my gut and believe that somehow it will work out. There aren't any right or wrong answers. Pick something you love and want to do and stick at it whether it takes six months or five years to get where you need to go. Don't compromise and work hard, and it will happen. Cheese over, put the cracker down.

Chris Wise

THREE

3

RULES
OF
THE
GAME

Grid systems

Every print design job is put together on a grid system. It is the grid system that is the underlying structure on which all design elements can be placed. They are an integral part of creating a recognizable rhythm—whether it be for corporate identity elements over a range of products or the consistency and flow in a book, magazine, or brochure.

For some companies, their visual identity and all its corporate elements within that identity are completely controlled by a corporate grid system. It is the indispensable, underlying structure, like the reinforced steel girders of a skyscraper.

Grid systems are most apparent in publication design, especially books. Wim Crouwel, when at Total Design in Holland, became one of the most famous exponents of the grid, creating striking and instantly recognizable formats to the extent his own nickname became *The Grid*.

When working on a new job that has had design work done before on it, always check what has been designed before for the client and take time to understand the grid system. It is like looking for the design DNA, and it will give you a deeper understanding of how you can approach the new brief.

Every design job has a grid system, however subtle or overt, and it is this grid that holds all the elements in place, page after page. It can be a very strong means to building visual recognition for a client, to the extent you could recognize or know the company the design piece is from, even if you cover up the logo.

The page opposite is not blank as some of the editorial team thought; it is a visual of the grid of this book.

This is a creative game—do not always do the expected

Typesetting

I could write a whole book on this as it is a vast subject with over a five hundred-year-old history of develovpment and experimentation. Now it is in the hands of young designers and their computers. It's frightening.

I fell in love with type because the letterforms had been beautifully drawn in a multitude of different ways and all I had to do was arrange them, working with these jewels with the precision of a gem cutter.

It used to take a compositor (the person who sets type) five years to become fully trained in the art of typesetting. Now, after a little formal training in typesetting, the responsibility is in your hands.

I spend most of my time trying to beat the computer at its own game. I know how I want the typesetting to look, and I fight the computer to get what I want, not what it wants to give me. I can set to a standard and detail so people believe it has been set in metal three-dimensional type rather than a computer.

Good typesetting is a craft and skill set that you will spend your whole career trying to master.

There is very little design where type does not make up over 50 percent of the graphic communication. So learn to use it like you learned to walk or ride a bike, as you will always need to be able to control it. Good type makes or breaks a job.

You are visually trained, so look for examples of good typesetting work and see how they have been done. Then get your setting to look the same.

I still buy books just because I think that the type looks brilliant. I explained to an antique bookseller, whose catalogs were appallingly typeset, that they

Read *First Principles of Typography* by Stanley Morison and apply the discipline to all that you do.
Bruce Nivison

Always be bold, take medium risks, make light of problems, extend yourself and condense your thoughts
Andy Lawrence

would do a lot better by picking any book off their bookshelves and copying the standard of setting in them instead of the crap they were producing. I think my honest straight talking in this case lost me that design job; I cannot as a visual person understand how you can look at beautifull typesetting all the time and then produce absolute visual rubbish.

You are visually trained, so look for examples of good typesetting and see how they have been designed. Typography may have hundreds of rules, but by the nature of its long history, nearly everything has been done well at some point. So find these pieces and study the font, style, size, kerning, and grid to learn what works well together. Then experiment and work out how to copy it, to get your setting to look the same.

The digital world has removed all the constraints and disciplines that have governed typography for over five hundred years.

This means that, as digital designers, your relationship with type and typesetting will need to be developed with a new discipline and attention to the beauty of detail. This will ensure that typography does not go down the watery way of anyone-can-do-it desktop publishing.

visually

Do the basics really well. Good type skills and a strong understanding of information hierarchy will go a very long way.
Joseph Luffman

My first real paid job as a professional designer in New York was at Fortune magazine, obtained after much difficulty during the bleak depression of the late fifties.

On my second day I was asked to design a small rubber stamp to dress up the envelope of a direct mail piece. The design was of a pointing finger. While doing the mechanical artwork and specifying the dimensions the telephone rang. While I was talking, the printer rushed in and snatched the mechanical from under my hand.

A week later I arrived at work to find a huge parcel on my desk with what I assumed to be a beer handle [tap]. This, I thought, must be a nostalgic gift from a friend in the old country. Wrong.

On opening the parcel I found a rubber stamp of a pointing finger 3', rather than 3", long. Obviously because of the telephone interruption I only got in one tick instead of the two.

Wracked with embarrassment I cradled the monster and took it in to my boss. I thought I'd be fired,

He laughed and hung the pointing finger from the ceiling of his office for a year.

Alan Fletcher, 1994

Make the idea bigger and the type smaller.
Lee Coomber

justify

My first rule is based on the fact that typography should actually be readable. Don't forget that you are young, and your eyes are near to perfect, so it is hard to understand why people have trouble reading five-point type—which to you is perfectly readable.

Point sizes can be misleading, especially when digitally rendered. If you look at 11-point Caslon, a serif face, against a sans serif face such as an 11-point Gill Sans, they are very different in readability. Don't just rely on the point size of type; always use your visual sense to judge the correct size for a font.

When typesetting on a computer, the size of the type is still referred to in a point size, even though these are not always the same as traditional type measured in points. You may find that a 12-point, hot metal is the equivalent to 12.25 points on a computer to give you the same visual outcome.

Using a long measure makes it very hard for the eye to come back to the beginning of the next line of type, however if you do need to cope with a long line length, the legibility of the type can be helped by more leading between the lines.

A very good rule of thumb is to actually read the text you have set to see if it reads easily. Remember that conventions change depending on which country you are in. Americans use double quotation marks while British stick with single ones, for example.

Do not try to justify type in very small measures (a measure is the horizontal width the type sets to); this is because it will either look too gappy between the words or need too much hyphenation to work well.

Another trick when setting justified text is to turn off the automated hyphenation and to add it

aligning

manually. This means you get to see how it sets and not allow the computer to make decisions for you. You can control the hyphenation style and amount of atomization by keying in the info onto the program's style sheets—however, I still don't trust it. I like to make my own decisions.

Always use *soft* hyphens (forces a line break in awkward places within text). This means that when the text changes, the hyphen will disappear if it's no longer needed.

If you are setting a traditional serif in an OpenType font (all have aligning and non-aligning figures), then you should use non-aligning figures as these were originally designed to have ascenders and descenders just like the rest of the characters in that font, that go up and down with the text, making it flow and easier on the eye to read.

Aligning figures were primarily brought about for sans serif fonts. If used in general text, they look like four capital letters, which stops the eye from reading on as easily.

If you set a line of capital letters in any font, look at the inter-character letter spacing: they will always need extra kerning to some extent with particular letter combinations.

These smallest attentions to detail can turn a piece of typography into a beautifully crafted design that is a pleasure to read.

Typography may have hundreds of rules, and some of those rules have become beliefs over time. The only rule in my book is, does it work visually?

Beliefs in type can be very dangerous, as all the constraints that controlled it for the past five hundred

years have now gone. With digital type on a computer
you can now do anything you want. After all, everyone
believed the world was flat for hundreds of years.

Don't be scared of breaking the rules, but learn the
trade beforehand and do it because you want to
and you have made your own judgment about it, not
because you didn't know something.

Also, with serif fonts, putting in ligatures is essential.
A ligature occurs when two or more letterforms
join together into a single graphical unit. Some
combinations of letterforms are naturally tight when
set together, for example fl or fi, and can look untidy.
In these cases we use ligatures.

Ligatures come from the days of hot metal typesetting
because certain combinations of characters did not
fit nicely together, creating gaps within a word. To
solve this, special characters were joined and placed
on a single piece of metal for use instead of two
separate characters (see page 125).

Ligatures are now specially designed glyphs, occurring
in OpenType fonts, which look much neater and are
designed so that each character does not interfere
with the next.

beliefs

Received a call from a multinational corporation to attend a briefing in Holland. We have a company plane, they explained, that will be ready to leave Gatwick at 8:30 am on Monday morning. Be there. Staggered out of bed at 5:00 am, too late for coffee, took a taxi to Victoria station, a train to Gatwick, arrived at the check-in desk, was conducted to a mini-bus, and arrived at the open door of an eight-seater corporate jet. A hostess with a clipboard raised a smile and asked my name. Odd, she said, there are already two on board with that name and the plane is full. The explanation was overbooking. Someone had assumed there was only one Fletcher, and that the three different people were one and the same. Returned to the terminal, the train, the taxi and got home for breakfast. Phone call to the client. Sorry, and all that, come tomorrow on a regular flight. Be in Eindhoven at 2:00 pm.

Up again at 5.00 am, too late for coffee. Taxi to Heathrow, ran to check-in desk, whisked off to plane. Sorry, announced the air hostess, no coffee—it's only a short hop. Rushed from plane to taxi. Was deposited at Rotterdam railway station. Bar open but train just about to leave. Into train—no buffet. Arrived at Eindhoven, saw cafe but was running late. Jumped into taxi. Arrived at headquarters. Rushed up to executive boardroom (it was just after lunch) full of replete suits finishing cigars over empty coffee cups. They got down to business. Once finished it was pointed out that I could make the last flight back to London—if I was quick. Down in the lift, into a taxi to the station…you've got the story.

Arrived home after midnight. Had a strong coffee. Couldn't sleep all night. And swore never to travel more than 50 miles without staying the night or leaving the previous day at the client's expense.

Incidentally—I never got the job.

Alan Fletcher, 1994

The importance of designing to the correct size

Once you know the actual size of the piece you are working on, and before you go very far (in the design process), always print out a first rough at the same size the actual item will be. You cannot judge size, typefaces, and layout on a computer screen. The final job, unless it is digital, will not appear on a computer screen but be printed in some format.

You have to get a visual of what you are making design decisions upon; I cannot stress enough how much time is wasted by not doing this. Do not ever trust the computer for this.

If after designing for thirty-five years, and using Apple Macs for over twenty years, I can't judge it, I'll guarantee you can't judge it very accurately either.

I once was having one of those discussions with a marketing department that kept telling me that the type was too small, and insisting it was enlarged, and that I was wrong.

Balls to that, I thought, so I printed out a section of it tiled on to 16.5 x 11.7" sheets, as it would actually appear when used, on a wall at an exhibition in this case. Having joined up the twenty sheets of the section, I rolled it up and went around to their offices. As I unrolled it and they could see the type was large enough to read from across the other side of the room, I chirped up, *If you can't read that, someone here needs glasses.*

I don't like marketing departments who seem to think they know more about design than the designers, and what they think is of course better than the mere designer. The best marketing people get on with what they know—marketing—and work in a partnership with the designer to get the communication across.

We live in a visual world and you have to look at design elements visually as they will be appearing *in situ* and real life.

You can judge neither type size nor color of type for printed matter by looking at the screen. Do not trust the computer—it misleads you visually. Print it off at each stage, because it's a process of refinement, like refining a recipe, until it works perfectly.

Designers do not spend long enough looking at the type before they say, that will do—it's only the type.

Type is the bedrock of graphic design. Good type looks effortless, it's a craft you need to master; the attention to detail will make a great job an award-winning one.

detail

The importance of designing with a pencil and paper

You will be used to designing everything on a computer, so today pencil and paper may seem like an old-fashioned way of working.

Designers in the pre-computer era (yes, there was design before computers) like myself only had pencils, ink, and paper to design with.

John Gorham, a brilliant English design thinker, made an advert for his design problem-solving skills. He took design back to its purest essence by using a simple photograph of the back of the envelope with a pencil. Under the envelope it read, *my only gizmo (computer)*, and under the pencil it read, *and its mouse*. The only other bit of type on the advert was his contact details. The poster failed to get him any work, but despite this it is still a brilliant piece of communication.

You can design faster with a pencil and paper than a computer. I will often stand with an author of a large book and draw out the flat plan, laying out the whole book in front of them as I am told which picture is important and which is not. This showmanship does amaze clients; it's like visual shorthand design. The teamwork and relationship you can build through this process is appreciated by the author.

You cannot do this as quickly if you were using a computer. Don't get me wrong—we were one of the first design companies to have a computer, way before most London design companies. So I have fully embraced them since day one; but they are only a great design tool.

Also, when doing first roughs for symbols or logotypes, it is faster to use a pencil and paper. I am chasing the raw ideas, not the finished visual. Only after the studio has discussed the concept and looked

As an experiment,
just try to
complete a
design without
a computer—I
guarantee you will
learn something.
Vyv Thomas

at the pencil roughs do we then work them up on a computer. **A computer will not give you an idea or concept**, and I believe that the standard of a lot of design has gone down due to designers relying too much on computers.

Young designers seem on the whole to be designing only to the level their knowledge of using a computer allows them to go. They are unable to visually think or design past their computer skill set.

A pencil sketch can get the client to see a concept and buy into the raw idea, whereas a finished visual does not give the client anywhere to go apart from whether they do or do not like it.

If it is too finished, the client is not involved with the process and will perceive the concept as finished.

You have to find a way to get a non-visual person to express themselves, and a pencil sketch can often help them do this, as they can see the base idea and have their ideas input into the process.

The quote below, while often cited, is actually factually incorrect, but I love the essence of it.

**NASA spent
millions to develop
a pen that would
write in space,
whereas the Soviet
cosmonauts used
a pencil.**

*The best design
software is
between your ears,
so keep it upgraded
by looking, reading,
and questioning,
and learn to think
with a pencil in
your hand.*

Andy Gossett

You have to be prepared to lose a lot of the creative input you had during school. In the majority of cases, as a junior you'll be working under a middleweight designer, senior designer, creative director, or a combination of these, and so really you end up just being a bit of a Mac monkey for the most part.

You're given opportunities to shine and come up with your own ideas, but it's rare that you'll truly get something to call your own, be able to put it in your portfolio, and say, I did ALL of that.

Maybe that's just me and I'm dumb for expecting more, but that's the main difference I personally found between the creativity at college and the creativity upon starting off in the industry.

Don't let failures get you down.

I'm pretty sure all of us at one stage or another had multiple really positive interviews (and even job offers) that were, for one reason or another, withdrawn at the last minute.

It's tough to not get your hopes up when people are so positive about you and your work, but everything that happens is an experience to learn from and take forward to the next opportunity.

Learn from any mistakes you made and don't let anything get to you, because sometimes a lost job opportunity is more about them and not you.

Alex Vissaridis

> **Work harder than anyone else. Never stop learning, exploring, and experimenting. Remember, being OK is never OK.**
> Giang Nguyen

If you have read and followed all the stages in this book so far, you should be making professional presentations already.

Your interviews are nothing more than your first presentations. You have learned how to put your work into a logical order, what to say, and what you are using to explain it. You are selling it to another person; there is no fundamental difference to this set of events when you start working for a design studio.

Each design studio will have a different flavor of the same popsicle. Some will present purely on a computer screen or by projecting PDFs. Others will flip through a portfolio presenting their work.

Your first task is to find out how the studio you work for wants it done. It may be three-dimensional mock-ups where you apply the graphics or brochures and mount the pages back to back to form a representation of the finished brochure. With the ability to print on both sides of a sheet of paper, you only have to worry about the imposition of your presentation.

Your craft skills are also important when putting together a presentation. Make sure the scalpel has a new blade and always used the full length of the blade, not just the point. Take your time, as it has to be cut out perfectly.

When you are printing your presentation, print it with tick marks as this avoids printing key-lines. If you're not very accurate with a scalpel, practice until you are.

Always cut against the steel edge of a ruler as this protects your fingers. If you do by mischance cut your finger, immediately move it away from the work. I do not want your blood on my presentation! Be

already

careful when using spray adhesive; sticky mock-up presentations do not look professional. If you are mounting your presentation onto foam board, when showing it to the client keep the design face down and order the presentation accordingly.

You have to be in control of the presentation, showing visuals and determining what the client sees and when.

Always double-check that you have the right presentation for the right client.

In the eighties, during incredibly busy periods in which I had to travel internationally a lot to meet the clients, I would get off one plane and board another immediately. In that space of time I was handed my new airline ticket and another portfolio with the presentation in for the next client, then proceed to check onto my next flight.

There was one occasion where I was sitting on the plane, en route to the next client, when I discovered that the presentation I had been handed was for a completely different client.

In the end, I had to do a lot of fancy footwork to move the meeting back, giving me the time to have the correct presentation flown out to me.

Always check and double-check you have everything you need so you never get caught in a situation like that. Another easy mistake is turning up for a meeting and having forgotten the client's full name. You have been so busy making sure you got the work done and arriving on time, you forgot the file with their last name in it.

The color-matching system

No one sees color exactly the same way. When choosing colors for printing, the same color can look completely different when viewed in two different manifestations and on different stocks, such as gloss, matte art, silk, and uncoated papers. This can be a tricky minefield, which is why there are color systems in place to control color choice from the computer menu on screen.

The color you are looking at on screen is backlit, and this projected color will therefore not give an accurate enough representation of what it will look like when it has been printed out onto paper.

Color swatches give you and the printer a fixed visual point, which you are both trying to achieve.

It is simply the visual look, intensity of color, that is the difference between how a color appears on coated and uncoated stock. You may find you even have to change numbers to get the best visual match between a color when on coated stock and an uncoated match.

When choosing a color from a swatch book (whichever color system it may be), always have an up-to-date book to ensure accuracy as colors will fade over time.

For the corporate colors of large businesses, it is imperative that their color looks the same every time it is seen; this means it must work well across different media. For example, it must work on screen, when projected, and on the web, as well as have consistency across all printed items.

With some large corporate identities that I have designed, like VISA, I commissioned a company that specializes in formulating a tailor-made set of color references to ensure that the proportions of the

ensure

CMYK ink mix are adjusted and refined to achieve exactly the same color across the range of different stocks that will be used within their corporate literature. Once I had chosen from a set of color tests on different stocks, I then approved a customized ink mix for each stock type. Swatches were then printed, notating the breakdown of the ink mix. These customized swatches were then used instead of Pantone swatches. Effectively what the client ended up with was a personalized corporate color specification, and printed swatch examples that now act as a guideline for all future print work.

Color systems exist to maintain control and consistency in the reproduction of color, which is the primary concern in design and for design-related professionals. Systems allows for people to speak the language of color across a variety of industries. It is worth bearing in mind that other continents may have their own specific color-matching systems.

PMS—UK—Pantone Matching System

The color system in the UK is the Pantone Matching System. Originally developed in North America, it is used so that when you choose and specify colors in your design work, the printer will have both a visual of the color you want and a given percentage breakdown of CMYK proportions to mix the ink into.

Pantone was founded in 1963 by Lawrence Herbert, and today the name is known globally as the standard language for color communication from designer to manufacturer to retailer to customer.

The Pantone number has a letter C, showing how it will look on coated papers, a letter U for uncoated and a letter M for matte. So make sure you always choose your color from the relevant section of the Pantone book, i.e., the section of the book that is printed on the type of paper stock you will eventually be printing on.

NCS—America—Natural Color System

The color system in America is the Natural Color System. The aim of Dr. Hard, the founder of NCS, was to create a color system based on how humans perceive and experience color. It was officially launched in 1979 and was published as a Swedish National Standard for color.

NCS is based on the six elementary color perceptions of the human vision, the psychological primaries (white, black, yellow, green, and blue). The colors are defined by three values: the amount of blackness (darkness), chromaticity (saturation), and the hue (the percentage value between two of the colors red, yellow, green, or blue).

DIC—Japan—Dainippon Ink & Chemicals

DIC is a *fine chemicals company* that works to bring *color and comfort by chemistry*. They first published their color book in 1968.

Their sample book has over 1,200 numbered colors, which have been organized in categories such as bright, showy colors and quiet, subdued colors to make it easier for users to pick colors that match their concepts. A number of themes have also been developed such as *Japanese Traditional Colors*, *French Traditional Colors*, and *Chinese Traditional Colors*. The system is mostly used for spot color matching, primarily in Japan.

RAL Classic—Europe —(*RAL stands for some ridiculously long and unpronounceable German name*)

RAL is mainly used for varnishing and powder coating

and today as reference for panels for plastics. In 1927 the Germans created a set of forty colors called *RAL 840*. Before this, customers and manufactures had to send each other samples to describe a color. RAL delivered numbers as color references making the process a lot easier. A new system was developed in 1933 for architects, designers, and advertisers based on CIELAB color space and used seven digits to define the hue, brightness, and saturation.

F2–595—Federal Standard 595—United States

Created in 1965 and dating back to World War II, it was developed by the U.S. government to standardize color specifications sent to international military contractors. A bit like RAL, it is a collection of colors (not a color space). It takes a set of color shades and gives each a five-digit reference number, instead of a name. Different to RAL and NCS, it is built in a color space model, which makes it a lot more flexible.

The first digit indicates sheen: 1. gloss, 2. semi-gloss, and 3. matte. The second digit defines the color group and the third to fifth digits refer to the intensity: lower number values mean darker colors and higher values lighter colors.

FOUR

GOOD
DESIGN
PRACTICE

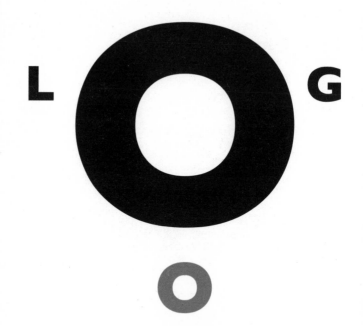

**Branding is not a
logo. It's a system.**
Leland Maschmeyer

Logo design in black and white

When you first start designing a brand identity or corporate identity, I would always first work in black and white, pencil on paper.

I would never start design sketches on **a computer**; the computer will not aid your ideas but, in my opinion, only curtail them. No matter how good your computer is and your skill set on it, it **won't ever give you a concept**.

Concepts come from you. What you feel and can conceive is a gift out of your own body and mind— it's your own unique and different way of looking at things. It is well worth remembering that the answer always lies in the brief, and it is the brief that will act to keep you focused on the problem at hand, while you're exploring your own creativity around it. You will be able to see your concept *naked* in black and white as there is no other distraction. The bottom line for any visual identity is how well it works in black and white; it is the lowest common denominator. It is also the purist point.

The general rule is that if it works well in black and white it will look even better in color.

The color can then be used to add more information you wish the visual identity to communicate.

If you find that an identity system works only in color, it is almost certainly too limited in its applications to do its job properly.

If the mark is not strong in black and white, it is also not going to work well in a newspaper or with cheap photocopying—a visual identity has to work brilliantly at the lowest common denominator.

Anyone who doesn't make mistakes doesn't make anything.
Stuart Newman

Design is valued and priced on the time it takes to do the job: how long it takes to design and complete a job multiplied by the hourly rate. Once a fee for a design job is agreed, then it is up to the designer to produce the correct result in that allotted time. It is a gamble, as certain jobs take longer than you imagine, in which case your hourly rate effectively gets lowered. It's rare to do a job quicker and find your earned hourly rate has increased.

So therefore it is important to always keep in your book a list of what time it took to do what job. Day to day, in most design companies you will have to fill out a time sheet so they can track jobs and ensure that they are on budget.

Also, writing in your own book at the end of every day the actual amount of time a job takes gives you an understanding of your own output. It is also a good idea to record as you go, because it helps with checking and filling in your actual timesheet.

Relax. It will take you as long as it takes you to do the jobs you have been asked to do. It is better that they are 100 percent correct than quick and riddled with mistakes.

Everything will take time to learn. The more you do a task, the easier it becomes and the quicker you get at doing it.

You're just starting out, so acknowledge the fact and have patience with yourself. If it's bothering you, ask if there is a quicker way of doing something. People will always help; you're all on the same team after all.

Remove the headphones and unplug the computer. True inspiration comes from life. Real life. Not some pixelated version of it. And remember, it takes interesting people to produce interesting work.

Sir John Hegarty

Producing work under difficult circumstances

There will be times when the situation you are in puts you in a difficult position with the work you have been asked to produce.

The main one is deadlines, having to come up with ideas against a ticking clock. This can be very hard, but it does get easier with experience. Some people only work under great pressure. Brian Grimwood used to order a bike delivery to take the finished illustration to the client, and then he had the time the bike took to get to him to finish the illustration. This is the sort of pressure he loved, but you have to be exceptionally skilled and confident to play that game.

I know I will find the answer to the design problem. It will come to me. I do my most creative thinking lying in a hot bath at 4 AM when I get up, but you have to have the forward planning to put the problem into your brain in advance.

Read the brief and then re-read the brief. The clue to the answer of any design problem is in the brief. If the brief does not explain the problem properly, then you can't solve it. It may also mean the brief is rubbish and wrong. I am renowned for redefining the brief so it actually says what the communication problem is. If the brief is bad, the design work will also be bad. If you can't define the problem, you can't design the resolution to the problem.

Always ask for help. You are a junior designer and if you can't crack the problem in the allotted time, tell someone. Design is a team sport. Ideas come from all over the place. Do not just sit there stuck; that isn't going help anyone. It will just slow up the whole design process. Ask and you will receive.

Always do what you are asked to, even if you think it is wrong. Then you do your own solution to hopefully

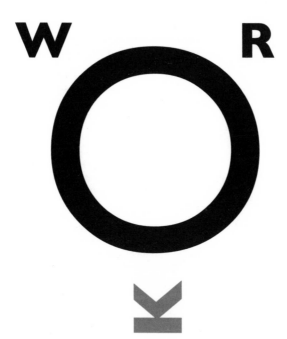

Learning to express your love for your craft will endear you to others.
David Brodie

awkward

Were I come from in London, when you speak you drop the letter h.

persuade someone to your way of thinking. You can only solve a visual problem with a visual; it is not an intellectual game, it is a visual one.

If a client insists he wants it done his way, I would show him what he asked for, then I would show what it should look like. In our game, visuals can solve problems quicker than words. You may not win the battle on a certain job, but the trick is to win the war.

Sometimes you cannot win the war. In which case you need to do the best you can do to find another client. Always be professional and put your all into a job even if you disagree with it. After all, it is only your point of view.

If you work with really awkward people in the studio, whom you just can't get along with, win them over or put up with them until you find another job. You can only hit your head against a brick wall for a certain amount of time before it hurts too much. Always take a deep breath, look at the long game and where you want to go. All the bad things end and life improves even if you think it can't.

Difficult circumstances can produce some amazing positive results in the end. Do not give up at the first hurdle.

The more hurdles you jump, the easier it gets to jump them. People expect to be able to do everything immediately, and consequently get frustrated with themselves when they can't.

You have just left art school; you forget how long it took you to learn to walk or how long it took to learn to ride a bike. It is impossible at the beginning, but once you have learned it you don't forget. Always remember how long your basic skills took to learn, and don't just give up.

The ability to juggle jobs

The ability to remember lots of tasks at the same time takes time, but learn it you must.

You can have multiple jobs with different tasks going on at the same time. The easiest way to manage is to always write notes about what you have been asked to do on each job. Always have a notebook; give each job a few pages and write a list of the tasks for each project. The main thing is to find out the deadline for each job or task you have been set.

Juggling jobs is like having ten plates on the top of long poles. As long as you keep spinning the poles the plates do not drop off. You run around spinning each pole just in time for it to not fall off, and be ready to dive to catch the one behind you if you forget.

If you only concentrate on the immediate task at hand, you might drop a plate because the next job may have needed something done on it—a phone call, a print quote, chasing an external supplier, etc. So when you get to do that task, always have your other tasks in the back of your mind and what you need to do for them.

Everything will take longer to do than you imagine. Estimating how long something takes to do and being precise about that time takes years of practice. When you are starting out, think of how long it should take you then double the time, and you're in with a chance.

Time will win if you play with it. Do not play with it. If need be, start the day earlier, work through lunch; working late is the last fall back position. If you do not stay ahead of time, it will really mess up your work and ability to keep on top of all your jobs. If you can, do anything and everything in your power to always be in front of time.

When you have evaluated your workload, and it seems you can't do it all, then make sure you tell the correct person that you can't do all the work in the alloted time and that you need help.

This will pass the responsibility back up the line to someone who has more experience in managing situations like this.

The earlier you shout, the more time there is to get out of the problem. It is the boss's job to make sure that it all works out in the end.

The importance of checking your own work

This is one of the best lessons to learn. It would seem obvious, but hardly anyone seems to be able to do it well. Check and then double-check your work. It is human nature to make mistakes, but to really foul up you need a computer.

If you have been given a task to do in a studio, at this point it becomes your job and no one else's. Once you have got it, it is yours, so own it.

At the start of your role on a job, check and double-check that you understand the background of the work. Not taking responsibility for your job and saying that you don't know, or that it's not your work, or that you didn't start it, or that you didn't know you had to do this, that, or the other are all lame excuses and just reflect poorly on you.

Before you show your work to someone higher up in the ladder, re-read the brief, check your work, and double-check it.

Every time you present your work and there is a mistake, it only shouts that you are not giving your full attention to a problem. When mistakes get into a job, and you don't find and correct them early on, you will chase these mistakes throughout the whole job.

No art director wants to spend their time continually pointing out mistakes. It is boring and slows the job down as well as reflecting badly on your focus and attention to detail. It is so easy to make mistakes. They are ready to trip you up all the time, and they will also multiply as a job progresses. So take care to check the work and double-check it as you go.

As a junior designer never send anything to a client directly without someone above you checking it. Make sure the designers who are briefing you check

Exceed expectations... especially your own.
Keren House

everything before you send out, however small it may seem. It is not your responsibility, and you do not have enough experience to take on sending work that is not first cleared.

It will only leave you open if something later turns out to be wrong.

Do not continually show someone your mistakes—it doesn't impress them. It's better to be slower and 100 percent correct than fast with loads of stupid mistakes. This is a team game.

Take the headphones off; you miss too much of what is going on in a studio if you retreat into your own world. Can you imagine a football game where all the players have got their own headphones on, listening to their own music?

Mistakes that are not picked up through not enough attention to detail, or by not engaging the gray matter, can easily end up in the final printed job.

Check, double-check, then check again. You do not want to spend your design life showing someone your inability to concentrate.

It's not just about good work, it's about *your* good work being seen. Lots of people have good work in boxes under the bed.
Andrew Baker

Do not trust what you see on screen when designing for print.

What to do when you first get a photograph

A designer's first instinct when starting the fun concept design phases of a job containing photographs is immediately to start designing and laying out the job. First do thumbnail sketches with a pencil and paper, as it's faster than using a computer, and get an idea sorted. After that the layouts will flow.

Check out the size you can use the pictures at, because the screen is very misleading. The pictures might look good on screen, but may be of no use as they are not a high enough resolution for printing.

When working with photographs and images there are certain steps you must take before designing anything.

No matter which file format you are using, you need to check the resolution and size of your photograph first.

To do that, open the image in Photoshop, go to image size, and uncheck Resample Image. That will link height, width, and resolution instead of only height and width. Now you can set the resolution to 300 DPI and figure out what dimensions you can work with.

It is important to do this right away, otherwise you might get halfway through a project and realize you can't print certain photographs or use them at certain sizes. This also ensures that you have a uniform resolution to work with so all pictures will look as good.

Nurture your self confidence… be brave and dare to think the unthinkable, because as creative people we demonstrate an uncanny ability to visualize what others can't see.

Phil Evans

But what is it that you're trying to become…a graphic designer…or a graphic communicator? Personally, I have never regarded myself as a Designer. I am a Graphic Communicator—because I create Big Ideas, not Designs. Surely, great graphic design is not merely the aesthetic arrangement of lines and shapes and typography—great graphic design is the transformation of a Big Idea into an unforgettable message!

In this astounding new world of technology, with tools that abound to help the graphic designer, they are meaningless without an essential idea. Without an idea, you are unarmed.

But be warned: the capability of your technical skills with a computer can never inspire the conception of a Big Idea. When an original idea springs out of a communicator's head, and intuitions, the mystical blending of concept, copy and art, whether in print advertising, TV commercials, posters, book design, magazine covers, editorial design, package design, logotypes, or websites, can lead to magic, where one and one can indeed be three. When that idea is dramatized by unique graphic imagery in synergy with words that memorably communicate in a nanosecond—there is always an immediate intellectual and visceral human response!

To be confident we can produce successful results as communicators, we must believe that an idea can solve almost any problem—because the creative act, the defeat of habit by originality, overcomes everything. Here's what I believe is the only way to become a great graphic designer: by creating Big Ideas and expressing them on paper, simply and powerfully with not one unnecessary line or shape, as well as having the courage to resolutely create only superb work through thick and thin and fight to protect it at all cost. Only then can you continue on a path to join the pantheon of the greats.

George Lois

FIVE

5

DESIGNER
RELATIONS

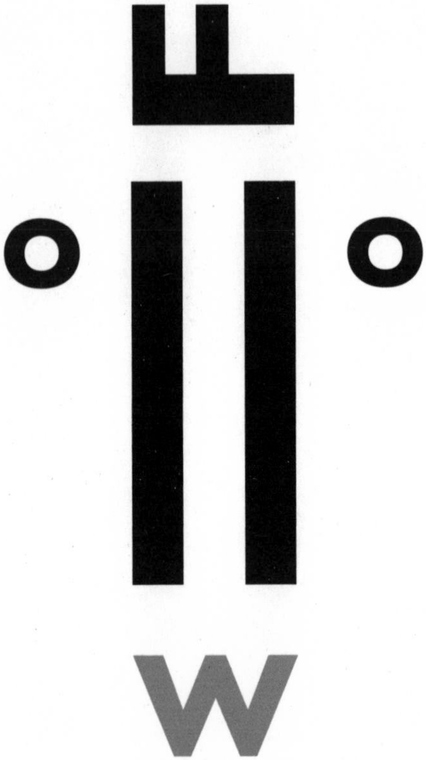

Simplicity avoids vainness.
Eiichi Kono

Now that you are in your first job, getting your feet under the table so to speak, keep abreast of news and who is doing what in your area of expertise.

I remember working freelance in Chelsea Manor Studios for a design company, and they had every copy of a graphics magazine going back to the first. This was a European glossy magazine of the graphic industry. I made sure I read at least five copies a week, just like a creative sponge absorbing water. You have to have a full sponge to continue producing great ideas and to stay abreast of what has already been done.

Read or look at what design work is being produced where. Follow the names on their websites. Having a job doesn't mean you can get complacent—you now need to keep it.

Join the different groups on LinkedIn and absorb and inform your mind continually. Keep the contacts you have made up to date. If you have done a great piece of work that you are really proud of, send them a copy of it, because it lets them know you're in the game and still interested in their firm.

Do not post work on your blog or send copies of work to anyone until the job is finished, and always ask permission first.

I once had a client ring me up, saying someone had stuck up on the web some of the rough designs of the job that we were doing for them. They were not amused at all as the job was under wraps until the big launch. The nice girl working as an intern with us had wanted to show her friends what she was up to. What she did not realize (nor did we in the studio) was that as soon as that client's name appears anywhere in the world on the web, they are immediately sent a notice of it. So be careful what you put up, as someone,

If you trust your
instincts, your first
approach can be
the best.
Julia Hasting

somewhere will notice it. Luckily, she wrote a brilliant
apologetic e-mail to the client, and they were very
understanding and let us off the hook.

Once a job is finished and out in the public domain,
it is fine to show what you have done.

Don't forget that, on the whole, design is a team
game, so never say that you designed something
without saying that you designed it while at work
or that you were part of the design team that
helped bring this about. You could always state
the responsibility you had in the team for this job.

Also never make false claims because you will get
found out at some point.

Design is a much smaller business than you realize.
For expample, John Spencer and I had designed a very
forward-looking visual identity for a bank in Greece
in the early eighties.

The whole concept was to use the Greek pattern.
I love selling people their own culture back to them.
It's of course a visual language, which as an outsider
you pick up on, but it is hard to see if you live there.
As John says, *I would and could sell snow to Eskimos.*

We had given the task, under strong art direction
of producing the identity manual, to one of our
assistants to carry out. When he joined Landor
Associates he was introduced as the man who had
designed the bank's whole identity. I think not.

found out

Experience: more important than grades

The game in design school is about getting the highest grades for your work and the highest score for your degree. It is the focus of your world at that time and quite rightly should be.

Once you have left, realistically no one will enquire about your grades again, because from then on it is all about your portfolio and will be for the rest of your working life.

Design groups use their portfolios to compete against each other to win clients. Their portfolios are always about the quality of work they have designed, not the quantity.

It is quality that makes you stand out in the crowd. Imagine you were a client: you wouldn't pick a design company that had a vast portfolio and lots of experience, but poor design skill and work. The same goes with you when you are applying for a job—only include your best work in your portfolio.

The portfolio is not only a visual presentation, it is also proof of experience. If you have a bit of time on your hands, make the most of it and develop your portfolio by taking on freelance work or competition briefs that will help tailor your portfolio more toward the job you aim to get. Just ensure you do not do this in studio time.

The more you are dedicated to achieving what you want to do, the more you will succeed.

In this industry, sometimes you will have to take on work that is very badly paid, but you know that in doing it, you will get a great piece of work for your portfolio. Other times, you will have to take on a job that is, and always will be, crap. In this situation, make sure that it is a very well-paid job, because it is the

> **Whether it's a high profile corporate ID or an in-house newsletter, approach the task with the same enthusiasm and determination for excellence. Adopt this attitude and you'll be in demand.** Mike Verdi-Cotts

portfolio

ABOUT

money that will help keep you going in the middle of the night!

I was once giving a lecture to a group of third-year students at a top Greek design school. I was told beforehand that the students' English and their understanding of it was not very good, so they would all need a translator.

One of the students asked how I had achieved my recognition and standing in the design industry. In answer to the student's question, I explained my *last man standing* approach; *I may not be the best, but I will outlast everyone. So by definition, just like being in a swimming pool, you will float to the top (just like something else!).* They all immediately burst into laughter. It turned out that their English was better than they were letting on.

The translator was too busy laughing to translate what I had just said!

If you're not having fun, you're not designing properly.
Phil Clements

If you are asked to design a piece of work for an existing client the studio has a current contract with, you should always refer back to files and get all the information on what the design work for this client looks like.

Designers may not be the best at briefing you on a job, because they assume that you know more about the job than you could possibly know, so just always remember to ask.

Study what that company has designed for the client before: what typeface, what size, the visual language, and work out if there is a house style. Ask for the files of previous jobs so you can access all the information you need before starting a job with a pre-existing client.

Everything that a company has designed will be in that studio. Don't come up with excuses like, *I didn't know it had to be like that* or *I wasn't told about that.* In my opinion, those excuses are lame. Get off your butt and find out all you can about the client's history, as it contains all the clues and visual answers that you will need for designing the next piece of work for that client. This job is not rocket science; there is a large degree of common sense. So please use your head and put *common* back into *common sense*!

Always ask questions of colleagues; there is no point re-inventing the wheel. *I don't know* is no defence. If you don't know, then go and find it out. You have to make yourself irreplaceable. If they start wondering what they did before you arrived, it means you're on the right track.

Your first client, in one respect, is your design studio and its designers. The work has to get passed through them before it actually gets to the client. Study how

The solution comes from understanding the problem.
Alan Fletcher to Vyv Thomas

that design company works, as it was their approach and style that first attracted the client and landed that studio the contract.

If you come up with a very radical approach to the work, however good it is, it is not likely to be used, because ultimately the client wanted the approach of the design studio you are working for, not the approach of a new individual.

Always design to the best of your talent and get what you have been briefed to work, no matter what you think personally. However, if you think you have a much better concept or approach, then stay late that night and do your alternative answer. Show this with the designs you were asked to do, and then go on to demonstrate what your concept or design is and how it answers the brief and works better.

This is what I look for. The key is a thinking designer. I don't just want Mac monkeys, I want designers who think and disagree with me, who can show me the error of my ways, by discussing all the aspects of a design job. In doing this, we all end up with a much better design solution.

monkeys

explaining

Explaining visual ideas to non-visual people

You have already got a skill set for presenting, as you started this at design school when you had to present your ideas to the rest of the class. Now you are presenting to designers and clients to get a job.

You are well-versed in presenting so it's not something that should bother you.

To explain a visual problem you need a visual. It is a visual game that you are in, not an intellectual one. You need the client to understand, and to be amazed at your skill set and your ability to think and resolve their communication problem. You need the clients to become part of your thinking and design process.

People look at Piet Mondrian's paintings and don't really understand a few black lines, a red square, and a gray one. However, if you look at all his paintings and put them in a line from his earliest to his celebration of New York, *New York Boogie Woogie* (1942–43), you can see how he has progressed from painting realistic images of nature, continually refining them picture by picture and over time, to the point and logical conclusion of that progression that we know and love today.

Take your non-visual person through a similar visual exploration. Get them to buy into their own work and let them see it unfold in front of them. Always start with the key points of the brief. Always pull out the benchmark qualities that were agreed before starting to design. Explain that everything they look at must be judged by the qualities.

It doesn't matter if you don't like the color; it is more important that it answers the benchmarks. If so, then I'm sorry, but it is correct! You may have to fake personal approval in meetings with the clients in order to sell an idea.

Show the visual process you have gone through, step by step. I often annotate mine so that if a client takes the presentation away and looks at it again later, or shows it to a colleague to ask their opinion, the annotations explain what is going on for each visual.

It is all about controlling the communication, so you need to make sure the presentation does this without you having to be there to explain each stage.

It helps to draw a flat plan of the presentation, so you can work out each stage of the design according to what the client needs to see and understand from the presentation.

Then design each element straight onto the presentation to save you having to rework and reorganize your work from a separate program or working art board—it saves having to do a job twice.

You are in the design game, so naturally as a designer you should always think of what you want to end up with at the beginning of the job, not at the end.

Never go into a meeting without working out what you want to achieve from it, as it is your job to guide and point the client in the direction you want to take them.

visual

Managing client expectations

We all know the disappointment when you have imagined something and the reality comes nowhere near close to what you want, or it doesn't do what it is meant to.

Or when you purchase something online, and the delivery does not quite match what you had in your head.

If you relate to these feelings being negative, then the last thing you want to do is having a client go through it. If you oversell your creative ability and what you can do for the client, and you can't pull it off, you are in trouble.

So managing clients' expectations is about communication and mentally standing in their shoes. Think about being on the other side of the desk and how you would react to what you are being presented with. The more you go the extra mile to achieve the right result, the more it will be noticed by your client.

Don't tell them the work will be ready at a certain date then not deliver. Get the quotes right; don't keep asking for more fees because you didn't work out the quote correctly. It is better to charge more, and then if you have come in under budget, offer the money back. That's a nice surprise for the client. Nobody gets upset with getting something back, but to constantly ask for more at every turn of a design job just pisses off the client.

The more you explain, and the client understands, the more relaxed they will feel. Hiring a creative and paying them to come up with that they want is not an easy, relaxing thing to go through from the client's point of view. It is potentially full of lots of unseen pitfalls.

relax

**Approach every
design project in
your career as
though it were
your last.**
James Alexander

At the start, tell the client stage-by-stage what they
are going to get (see pages 195–199). It's all about
communication; don't let them misinterpret what
they are getting. Once you've told them what they
are getting, tell them what they have got.

I once had a set of very bad proofs for an important,
very expensive job. I got the printers to pull out all
the stops and the next set was brilliant. As it turned
out, too brilliant. While on press, they could not
match the second set of proofs. The proofs were
over-egged and impossible to achieve on press, and
the client that was turning up to see the job was
going to be very disappointed. The printer was saying
we should just tell them it's not possible to do what
we did on the proofs, but that would still disappoint
them. The printing was very good indeed, but the
perception was brought down by the proofs. So I got
all these second proofs removed from sight and when
the client arrived showed him how we had come from
the first proofs and how brilliant the final print turned
out. He left a very happy client.

Do not over-promise something you cannot deliver.
Keep a client updated on every stage of the job. Be
proactive: write meeting reports after every meeting
explaining what was agreed. It is always best to avoid
any chance of misunderstanding.

You want to deliver Rolls-Royce service whatever
the fee or client, and the customer is always right.
We may call them clients but they are customers
at the end of the day. I now spend my time trying
to convert customers into becoming patrons.

The process of placing type on a sheet of paper is in effect a search for the Golden Mean. The knowledge of how to go about it is essential for any good designer. This fact had not been made clear enough when I was a student, and curiously it is still not being made to students now. Frequently colleagues looking to employ new staff bemoan the scarcity of good designers. I felt this same lack throughout my career as a designer and art director. How can this be, when graduates leave college every year in droves? Why is serious typography still not an imperative on the curriculum of good graphics courses?

Phil and I were both studying graphic design at the Central School of Art and Design, now part of Central Saint Martins College of Art and Design. I, an eager student from Poland, Phil, mccoy London boy, endearingly substituting his 'ths with Fs or Vs. Margaret Fatcher (much in the news at the time, cutting student grants as Minister for Education) and Vat one not vee over one were Phil's solid gold quirky pronunciations which always made us smile. Both our accents were fondly embraced by our fellow students, who were essentially middle class and well spoken.

The school occupied a spectacular purpose-built building designed by William Morris's friend William Lethaby, who also became its first principal. Lethaby promoted break of distinction between applied and fine arts and such an outlook was reflected in the curriculum, also set by him. Thus crafts like typography, bookbinding, and silversmithing were fostered with a creative approach. This legacy still remains intact despite the school's amalgamation with St. Martins. The Central prided itself in employing some of the most important names in art and design, practicing artists and designers as well as part-time teachers and lecturers. On our course we were lucky to have eminent typographer and designer Anthony Froshaug. Anthony's slender figure, clad in a signature gray smock, narrow black trousers, and black desert boots itself resembled a ligature from a refined font.

**It's from the
heart and from
experience. It's
a plea for better
typography!**

It spelled Bauhaus. His hands were always occupied; a small black leather pouch in the left and in the right a pipe, which he used as a pointer. He was neat and precise. A Modernist, a purist. He built typographic pages as Mies van der Rohe built houses. Nothing out of place, nothing unnecessary in sight. His design was clean, transparent, full of light. Above all, considered and intelligent. The message was always clear in an instant. He taught us how to dissect text, extract the essence, make visual sense of it and disappear without leaving a trace. The projects he set us were analytical, involved, and slow. They were teaching us indispensable rules of this science. If only I'd been more aware of its importance at the time! We even had a working compositing room full of lead fonts, where we could try hand setting. This was Anthony's domain. Technicians in industrial, button-up brown overcoats busied over setting the college's yearly prospectuses. They also helped us. But this room was essentially for masters and apprentices. One had to be of a certain ilk to be able to do typesetting seriously. It demanded commitment and endurance, and most of us were far too arty and flamboyant to knuckle down to the minutiae of letter spacing and constant ink-stained fingers. However, Phil had what it took to commit to this fine-tuned craft. He became Anthony Froshaug's disciple and later cut his teeth working with some of the best names in the business, now legends of graphic design. Years later, to my delight, I heard that Phil Cleaver joined their ranks.

Eventually we all graduated and went our separate ways. Pretty soon after I fell into the glamorous world of glossy fashion, interior and Sunday supplement magazines. It suited me perfectly. Heading launches and re-launches of some major titles was exciting, as was working with world-famous photographers, illustrators, and stylists. However, having to form teams to execute these assignments, I quickly realized how difficult it was to find designers who commanded a good knowledge of typography. I myself thought I knew far too little, but I knew a bit more than those I happened to end up working with. I yearned for

Typography for a graphic designer: it's like knowing how to read or walk.

some expert help and advice. If someone displayed a flair for type, I quickly invited them to join the team. My art departments were always full of students, and typography students were most welcome, even if they didn't speak English! Such a mix provided a constant breath of fresh air to the full-time staff as well as being educational for all of us. During my ten-year spell at Conde Nast, by chance I developed an ongoing relationship with a college in Paris that provided a flow of graduates with master's degrees in typography. It was a pleasure to look at the layouts they designed. Sometimes they missed the point of the story and had to redo the layout, but the type always felt comfortable in its placement, it made sense, it was harmonious with the photographs or indeed suited the subject from the historical point of view. It was considered.

Work experience students would often ask me for advice on how to proceed in order to succeed in their design careers. My answer was always to do a serious typography course. Without it they would never be able to be confident in their design. Such knowledge gives the designer an ease of exploring different concepts. Bad type at a glance obliterates the best of ideas. Great type can save the day. For years I watched so-called designers pushing type around the page hoping for a lucky happenstance, for it to somehow fall into the right place. It was painful.

On a recent assignment in San Francisco I had to form a design team. Tutors from a renowned design college were kind to recommend a few star graduates. The online portfolios indeed looked interesting. I chose a charming young man, a technological whizz, a skill I much appreciated. However, during the first ten days, presented with having to design sample pages for a book, he displayed, to my total disbelief and his panic, an absolute lack of any skill as to how to go about it. Asked how so, he said that they, the students, had been taught that it was the great ideas and concepts that count and that everything else, like setting type, was to be left to

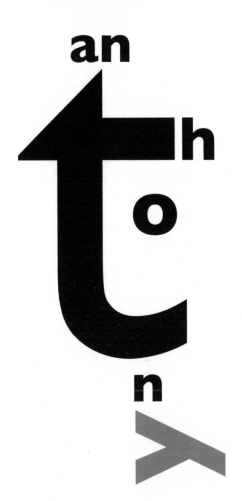

technicians. And, that when they became famous art directors, they would be employing technicians and telling them what to do. Apart from sounding ridiculous, the idea felt uneasy, as it insinuated that technicians were an inferior caste. This insane divide preached by the educators seemed unfair and harmful to the industry. The very divide that the enlightened William Lethaby, principal of the Central School of Arts and Crafts, as it was called then, sought to get away from over one hundred years ago. It is true that in large publishing houses there are typesetting departments that take care of fine tuning typography. But the designer has to have the knowledge too. Anyhow, many a discussion and friendly-though-heated argument later, I hope some important issues were brought to light and made these young designers realize their handicap. Needless to say, I opted for technicians—not a perfect solution either because, despite being brilliant and fast Mac operators, they in turn suffered a confidence problem relating to their lack of design skills. A lose-lose scenario.

This experience made me realize that the situation in the UK is much healthier. But the question remains: given that thousands of graduates leave graphic design schools every year, why is it that designers still lack serious typographic skills? I came across this fact just the other day. Again!

Watching type being skillfully placed in space is like listening to a beautiful choir. Phil's book will help you to sing in tune. Make sure it lives in your pocket.

Perhaps sometime in the future Professor Phil will give lectures on typography and its history. I would be the first one to attend.

Malgosia Szemberg

6
SIX

SOFTWARE
SKILLS

How to batch process images

Batch processing images is a great way to get the computer to do all the repetitive work for you, especially if you have to convert hundreds of images from RGB to CMYK to send to print or to make low resolution files you can then design with.

Basically, the computer watches exactly what process you go through with one file, and it records this like a film of the events.

Then you select the folder with, say, a hundred image files in, and it performs the exact same process to every file in that folder automatically.

So, take extra care! If you do it wrong while setting it up, you will end up with all the subsequent files being wrong.

The basics of how to do this are explained below.

This book is not meant to be a guide on how to use a computer, as that is covered in a multitude of ways elsewhere. It's here to make you savvy to industry ways of working.

There is so much that is readily and clearly available online, and this is a valuable resource at your fingertips.

What I will advise, however, is this: if you look something up online, or someone in the studio shows you in person, always write it down in your sketch book, so you'll know for future projects.

Before beginning your batch processing, make sure you have all the images you wish to batch process saved in one folder, and create a new folder the new versions can be saved to.

repetition

Then open one image in Photoshop and make sure the action window is showing (to do this click Window > Actions).

Press *record* in this window (this will record a new action) and proceed in carrying out the process that you wish to repeat on all other images in your chosen folder. Save this file, and then in the action window click *stop*.

The next step is to click File > Automate > Batch. A window will appear asking you to first choose your new action in a dropdown menu, then select the folder of images you wish to be batch processed and the folder the new versions will be saved into. Once you have filled in this information click *ok,* and the computer will begin batch processing all images in your chosen folder, saving you a lot of time and effort.

How to set up a style sheet

**Live and learn.
Studying in college
is just a synopsis,
real life practice is
a new chapter.
Learning from
the experienced
person is the
best way to grow
stronger.**
Siok Teng, Chan

The idea behind setting up a style sheet in InDesign is in essence the same behind using Cascading Style Sheet (css) on a website: it allows you to very quickly and easily change everything about a design aspect of what you are producing.

It saves time and effort, but more importantly it prevents human error. If you try to manually change every subheading, you might do one wrong, forget another, and the design no longer looks consistent. This tool is particularly useful when designing things like brochures or books, which need a consistent style throughout.

In InDesign this is done through Character Styles and Paragraph Styles. To do this, set up a page to look exactly how you want it to, then open the Character Styles window under Window > Styles. Select the relevant part of the text and click on the *create new character style* icon on the bottom right of the window. Paragraph Styles are set up in the exact same manner.

This is only a base guide; if you need more details there are many tutorials available online. There are two things you should bear in mind when creating your styles, though. One, always define the character styles first, because the paragraph styles will override them. Two, make sure you name the styles well. That allows you to keep track of what you are doing, particularly in long-term projects, and it makes it easier to pass the project along for anyone else who might join the brief or be working on it.

essence

example

How to set up masters in InDesign

A master page is created by default and acts as the background to all of the pages in your document. Anything you apply to the master page will be applied throughout. Master pages are used to apply page numbers, repeating logos, headers, and footers, as well as repeated guide lines, text boxes, and frames.

If you're not on the master page, then you cannot move anything around that has been placed on the master page (unless you override it by holding down Cmd-Shift and click on the object).

To view the master page, go to Window > Pages. The first master page is marked as *A-Master*. This is the main, default master page, also known as the *Parent Master*. If you click and drag the *None* page (above master page) then you can create a new page that isn't based on the master page. Every new master page you create will be named alphabetically.

You can create a new master, which is based on an existing master page. This is called a *Child Master*. Simply click and drag the master onto the *New* icon.

You would use this for a ten-chapter book. The parent master would be for the overall design, e.g., page number and book name. For each of the chapters you would use child masters. This would allow you to make small changes to each page, such as the chapter title. Any parts of the parent master that you don't want on the child master you can just override and edit by pressing Cmd > Shift > Click.

Nothing will prepare you more for your career in design than your first year in it.
Elizabeth Rogers

quicker

How to manage large volumes of text and images

When handling a large body of text in InDesign, it is quicker and easier to manage if you design the text frames on the master page before you place the text into your document.

Click on to the master page and draw your text boxes. Next, you have to link them together by clicking on the first box. At the bottom of text box there will be a small blue arrow (the arrow only appears once it is linked). Click this. The *Place Text* icon will appear and you click this in the top left corner of your next text box, and so on.

Go back to the first page of your document, go to File > Place, and select the relevant document (or Cmd+D). The *Place Text* icon will appear again and you click it in the top-left corner of your first text box and the whole document will spread over the other linked boxes throughout.

Large images will slow down InDesign, so to prevent this happening it is easier to initially work with images that have a lower resolution (72 DPI). When you have finished your document, you can replace these images with original, higher resolution images.

You can reduce the size through batch processing the images in Photoshop (see page 119). When you have finished your document, simply relink the images with the original file of the higher quality images.

The fastest way to do this is to move where the lo-res pictures are saved. InDesign will then show these links as lost. When you re-link one of these lost links with the high-res version, InDesign will re-link all of the pictures that share the missing link names in that folder.

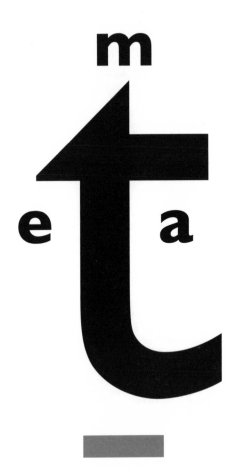

How to input ligatures

A ligature occurs when two or more letterforms join together into a single graphical unit. Some combinations of letterforms are naturally tight when set together, for example fl or fi, and can look untidy. In these cases we use ligatures.

Ligatures come from the days of hot metal typesetting, because certain combinations of characters did not fit together without creating gaps within a word. The letter f overhangs into the next space.

To solve this, special characters were joined and placed on a single piece of metal for use instead of two separate characters.

These are specially designed glyphs, occurring in OpenType fonts, which look neater and are designed so that each character doesn't interfere with the next.

An InDesign document can be set up so that ligatures are automatically included when the text is typeset. This can be done by clicking the *Type* tool in the tool palette, then clicking on the button furthest to the right on the taskbar underneath CS Live. This will produce a dropdown menu, and here you can click *Ligatures* to ensure that InDesign automatically includes all basic ligatures where they are needed. Each font will have a different number of ligatures. Some may have the full range available, while others may only have a few. Due to these differences, once your document is typeset, it is then worth going back through using the find and replace tool (Cmd+F) to double check that all ligatures have been used where they are needed.

All ligatures can be found in the glyph palette, which is found by clicking *Type* in the toolbar at the top and selecting glyphs.

compliment

Which file type for which job?

Imagine trying to slice a loaf of soft white bread using a hammer. Things would probably get quite messy. The same thing happens when you use the wrong file format on a design job—the result just isn't as beautiful as it should or could be. But there are lots of formats to choose from, so which is best for what?

When in doubt, ask your buddy Google first, and then secondly, ask someone you're working with, *Which is the correct format for this studio?* This implies you do know something (you have just googled it so you should), and it suggests you have a willing attitude and are ready to learn the way that particular studio would like its work done.

Every designer has had a first time in a studio, and being asked for help by a new starter should be seen as a compliment. But only ask once, and then write the answer in your sketchbook. Asking again only makes you look bad.

As a starting point, the key file formats and their primary uses are outlined here.

.tiff Prepress file format for raster data—photos, etc. A tiff can be created with a transparent background and supports multiple layers. It is used to supply raster images to printers (300 dpi, CMYK).

.pdf Adobe's attempt at a universal file format, **p**ortable **d**ocument **f**ormats are great for e-mailing designs/ portfolios/résumés and for supplying visuals and artwork to printers. A PDF is a flat file format. Refer to page 133 for more information.

.jpeg A compressed file format, for raster data only. Jpegs are used widely for photographic data on the web.

.ai   Adobe Illustrator's native file format, used for vector data: logos, illustrations, and so forth. This format is ideal for supplying designs to screen printers, signage companies, and other creatives. It also supports multiple layers.

.psd   .psd—Adobe Photoshop's native file format, supporting raster data. The psd format is excellent for photo editing and creating raster imagery. It can be created with a transparent background and supports multiple layers.

Whenever possible, avoid creating type in Photoshop as it is automatically rasterized and may appear pixelated as a result.

.indd Adobe InDesign's native file format. Great for layouts and publication design, from small leaflets to five hundred page books. This InDesign format is often supplied to printers packaged alongside a PDF.

.eps   A vector format commonly used to transfer design elements from one program to another, or to supply to another creative. Vector-based eps files are scalable to any size without compromising quality.

.png   A raster file format primarily used for the web due to the low resolutions supported. It can be created with a transparent background and is therefore excellent for web icons, buttons, and logos.

Do not forget the period or full stop

avoid problems

When to use CMYK and RGB and their differences

A very simple rule to learn: if the job is on screen, RGB is fine. Off screen it has to be in CMYK.

CMYK and RGB are the two color modes but have opposite mixing processes.

CMYK (cyan, magenta, yellow, key/black) is a reductive process and is the color mode for print.

RGB (red, green, blue) is an additive process that uses light on screens to create colors. There are over three thousand colors available on the CMYK color range; however, it is a much more limited pallet than the RGB Color Spectrum.

There are huge differences in luminosity between the two; the amazingly bright colors that you can use on screen are not all achievable in the CMYK print range.

When printed, colors are generally dimmer and darker in comparison to how they look on screen, so you have to be careful that if you're designing something for print, you are always working in the CMYK mode to avoid problems.

Checking and changing the color mode varies across the Adobe programs. Photoshop works in RGB by default. To change the color mode of an image, click Image > Mode > CMYK.

If there are large changes in color to your image then just adjust the Curves and Levels.

To set up a document ready for print in Illustrator, click File > Document Color Mode > CMYK Mode. You can also ensure that all the colors you use are available on the CMYK spectrum. If you double click the color icon in the tool bar, the *Color Picker* box will appear.

If the color you have selected is not available in the CMYK scale, then there will be a small box next to the *ok* button with a yellow warning sign above it. If you click the warning sign, your color will automatically be matched to the closest color available in the CMYK range.

In InDesign you simply click Window > Color to open the color box. In the dropdown menu, change the mode to CMYK. Any color you chose (even an RGB color) will automatically be matched and changed to CMYK.

When printing to the studio color printer, if you get a notice that says *Out of Gamut*, it means that the colors chosen are not CMYK.

If you have a photograph that you discover is RGB, simply go to Window > Links > Links Info, then right-click the image name and press Edit With > Photoshop. In Photoshop click Image > Mode > CMYK > Save. Keep an eye out for how the colors in the picture change—it may need some retouching after as the picture may become quite flat-looking from the color range loss.

simple

What program to use

If you can't draw cows' feet, stick them in a field of long grass.
Art teacher Janet Slade to Diana Chamberlain

Always ask which is the best program that particular studio uses. Normally you learn programs at school, so you naturally prefer one of them and use that one to do most of your work in.

Studios on the whole follow a system, which could be, for example, the base program is InDesign, and then any illustration is done in Illustrator and imported into InDesign, or any photographic context is done in Photoshop and also imported into InDesign.

Each studio will have its own way of doing things, so find out before you start any given job as to what the studio will want you to use.

Do not start the job in your favorite program without asking, as it will only really irritate and annoy the studio you're working in.

Freehand was our studio's base program for years; it was an amazing program for controlling type and drawing logotypes and symbols. The other one was Pagemaker. Illustrator eventually took over from Freehand. Pagemaker was written by compositors, whereas its rival Quark was written by programmers.

Pagemaker was an intuitive design program and Quark was, in my opinion, an artwork program. Pagemaker, or what is left of it, is embedded in InDesign.

You will probably have learned InDesign at college, which is the industry norm at present. If you have to use Quark, don't get worried, because it is very similar to InDesign. Just ask for help when you get stuck. You can convert Quark to InDesign through a program; however, do check what the studio wants you to do before commencing.

anon

How large can you blow up a high-res image?

It is very easy to be deceived by what you see on screen, and as a designer you may not take into account the enlargement because it looks great on your computer. The general expected rule is that when the high-res image is in your design program, you should not enlarge it over 120–130 percent. At 130 percent you're beginning to push it, but we have taken some up to 150 percent (depending on the image).

So as a general rule, never enlarge over 120 percent as it will ensure you won't get into trouble.

Always make sure you sort out the photography before you start designing with it. Check the resolution is 300 DPI in Photoshop first; getting all your content into the correct format will ensure you don't design things that look great but are impossible to print.

When images are being used as banners or something similar, the banner makers have software to help enlarge photography to higher resolution, but they only work in this medium and not litho printing.

preserves

Saving PDF files, which formatting, and PDF markings

Adobe PDF preserves the formatting regardless of the original application that created it, including text, video, drawings, and meta-data.

Saving a document as a PDF has a lot of advantages: it embeds fonts and images, displays in and prints from pretty much any computer in the same way, and greatly reduces the file size.

To save a PDF in Illustrator or Photoshop, just go to File > Save As and select Adobe PDF. There you can select which markings you want to show in your printed sheet. In InDesign, to save a PDF go to File > Adobe PDF Presets, and here you can choose whether you are saving for high resolution or simply lowest file size.

Crop marks show where to trim the printed sheet.

Registration marks are represented by a circle with a cross through it. It is printed using each color of the CMYK spectrum, and they should overlap perfectly. So if one of the colors is not aligned properly the off-set will show right away.

Color bars are printed just outside the trim marks. Used for quality control, they allow the printers to check the color's density and consistency throughout the whole document. This is sometimes automated with the use of scanners.

Page information contains the file name, page number, current data, time, and color separation names.

When to retouch a photograph

If you have the right photography or the right photographer you will not need to retouch.

The photographer should retouch his own work before he hands it to you.

Retouching is the last resort, not a starting point, though sometimes it is necessary and unavoidable. As a junior designer your Photoshop skills, *however good you may think you are*, are very unlikely to match those of a professional retoucher. So don't attempt it yourself. If you think anything can be improved always tell someone—it's your job—and after all it's up to you to get it to the best quality you can.

In a client meeting, what needs to be explained is you *can* clone out or remove an element of the photograph, but you must ensure you have a suitable part of the photograph to replace it with. You can't make something out of nothing.

It's up to you to study every photo as a fresh pair of eyes and comment on them if they can easily be enhanced. But never say it out loud in a client meeting; always suggest it to the person you are working with in the design company.

Design is always a team effort, but don't get picky just to get noticed.

picky

Scaling images

fit

Designers spend a lot of time going back to clients explaining that the images they sent are too low resolution for printing. The images look great on screen, so clients find this hard to grasp.

If the client doesn't have high-res images, they are not going to be good enough to print with.

The client either has to find a high-res file or get it re-photographed. If their files are not high enough resolution you can't do anything about it.

Images need to be scaled depending on their function. Smaller images, with lower resolution, are easier to send via e-mail so you would resize these to 72 DPI.

For print, they should not be lower than 300 DPI, otherwise their print quality will be poor.

You can batch process—see page 119—and scale down a file of images to 72 DPI by clicking Image > Image Size > Resample Image > Resolution 72.

In InDesign, you will adjust the size of your images to fit the design document you're working on, as you probably won't know which size you need until you place the images.

The quickest way to alter the image size is to tap E (no need to hold it down), then hold Shift + down while clicking on the image's corner. The frame and the image will scale together, rather than having to do both of them separately.

There are a few things you need to check in the *Links Info* panel after scaling an image. Click Windows > Links and select the image name. In this section you can see the percent you have scaled your image up or down, which also affects the PPI (and effective PPI).

For print, the PPI needs to be 300. If the image has a smaller PPI, then there are steps you need to take to change this.

Open the image in Photoshop from InDesign (for instructions on how to do this see page 129). Then go to Image > Image Size and uncheck the *Resample Image* box. Next you need to type 300 in the Resolution box and click OK > File > Save. This will change the measurements of your image to 300 DPI.

serve all

What makes great art, a great design, a great logo?

An artist should always consider the viewers and not him or herself when expressing their work. Our best foot forward is when we express on behalf of all rather than just seeking to show or bring recognition to the needy self.

Think humanity and you will think bigger than you can ever be on your own.

So think beyond and/or greater than your boss, your colleagues, your clients, for they too are all equally considered as you are when you express for the whole of who we truly are. A great creation must serve all, for if it does not, it is not as great as it is claimed to be.

Would anyone like to argue with Mona Lisa?

Serge Benhayon

SEVEN

PRINT PRODUCTION

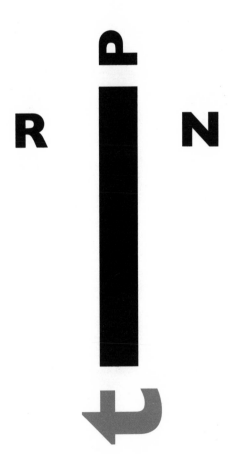

How to write a print specification

To get a quotation on how much something is going to cost to print, you will need to write a print spec. It is basically like a list of the ingredients in a recipe, and the printers bake the cake.

The relationship with printers is, in some ways, very similar to that of architects and builders. The designer is always trying to push the envelope, and the printer is wondering why you would want to print something that way.

The smart trick is when you have sent out three or four of the same quotes to different people, to very carefully read all the incoming printers' quotes as they may not be quoting like for like. You need the quotes exactly the same so you can compare their print prices against each other. The main headings you need are: title, finished size, content, colors, material, finishing, origination, delivery, quantity, and price.

If you have not seen examples of their printing jobs, always ask them to send a finished example closest to your quote so you can see the quality of their work and printing. It is like a designer showing their portfolio; printers will happily show examples of their work. You can use this to compare the quality and the pricing of different printers against each other.

Take note of which printer seems most helpful on the phone, who gets the quote back the quickest, and who's winging it. All these things will give you an understanding of what they will be like to work with.

Like designers, some printers are just awkward and unresponsive to work with. Life is too short, and there are enough printers out there for you to find a printer who likes working with designers and has an appreciation for the craft of design.

How to create an artwork for print

For the web, you program; programming is the actual artwork. If, however, your artwork is going to print, you check the printout because that's where you will see it—in a printed, rather than a screen, format.

Even quite experienced designers think if it looks good on screen then it's correct. This is untrue—you can only really judge design for print when you see a printout. When judging type in particular, only trust a printout.

If unsure about artwork for print, I would ask the printer, as it is his responsibility to produce the job.

Before you send off your design file for print, there is a checklist of points to go through and ensure your document is ready.

For your images, you need to check that their resolutions are no lower than 300 PPI, they are all CMYK, and that all spot colors have been noted for the printer. Ensure that all keylines have been removed. Check that all your images and fonts have been linked or/and outlined, and that everything is in the right place.

When you are creating the PDF, ensure all the bleed and crop marks have been included. Always check the PDF before sending it, because sometimes files can corrupt.

ensure

How to package a file and deliver to the printer

Now that you have done all the hard work, corrections on corrections, change upon change, check and double-check everything is correct. Get someone else to check it. Have the client sign it off.

You now have to get all the elements to the printer. Where possible, I always hand over a hard copy (digital printout) on which the client has signed his name as approval to print.

The printers then have something to check the work against. Computers do and have hiccupped, and that can be very expensive.

Never trust a computer—it's the only thing in life that's guaranteed to let you down.

Packaging a file ensures that all the links (fonts and images) are collected into one file. This makes sure you have all the elements of the job. In InDesign you do this by clicking File > Package.

The window that pops up shows a summary of your publication and highlights any missing links or uses of RGB (RGB is no good if you're going to print). If there are issues you will have to go back and re-link/change them.

When you have packaged the documents, you can compress the file to send it over to the printers. Also send a hard copy—so the printer can check that everything on your files matches the runout—and a color PDF.

Resolution versus scale

There is a difference between an image's resolution and scale, and it is important to understand this. Scale refers to the size of an image, the width and height. Resolution is the amount of pixels or dots per inch (PPI or DPI).

In InDesign you can click on the photos to see at what percentage they are scaled. On the links window you can see picture information, for example the actual PPI (the resolution of the image at one hundred percent) and effective PPI (the resolution of the image at the size scaled in InDesign), dimensions, and more.

There are ways to digitally alter an image to increase its perceived resolution and quality. However, this is specialist knowledge available from professional services and not typically used in studios.

When printing something larger than average, like a banner, you should ask the printer what they need you to send them since they will often use their own software to blow things up.

re**solution**

What is high res for print?

Just because a picture looks good on your computer screen, it doesn't mean that it will look good printed out. For printing purposes, printers need high-resolution pictures to be in TIFF format and CMYK.

If the original you are looking at has a low resolution, it will only look worse when printed.

Every step away from the original is, by very definition, a step in the wrong direction for quality.

Your final printed job will only ever be as good as the quality of the origination. Origination is the visual content of your job, i.e. the illustration/photography.

The picture has to be 300 DPI resolution and at a size that when imported into a design program is no more than 120 percent enlargement. So that means once you placed your photograph into an InDesign dialogue box, check the enlargement percentage by placing the white arrow on the picture and clicking.

Once you get a brown bounding box, look at your tool palette—the third one along to the right will have the percentage size displayed in the top and bottom slot. Check they are identical percentages. If not, your picture will have been distorted by the computer. Always check your chain program is not broken.

enlargement

How to use a color matching book

In printing terms again the computer is misleading. What you see on a monitor/screen is a back-lit, illuminated color; it's much different when looking at color printed onto paper, which has only overhead light to reflect the color back at you.

Ink swatches on different stocks—gloss, matte, silk, uncoated, etc.—show the real color that will appear when printed. The swatches also show how the same colors will look when printed from a full four-color set. This changes colors considerably.

When choosing any color in printing you must refer to a printed swatch to see what you will get, as it is a visual match you and the printer can use to ensure the color is correct.

When deciding on a corporate color for an organization, you have to check how the color appears in all media and not only on screen.

The accuracy of color in the design game is critical, so the colors all have a number and suffix (stock reference). There are over 1,100 unique, numbered colors. Pantone books are used to choose spot colors; each has their own mixing formula.

For example, a company will choose a spot color to be its identity like the green of the Heinz Baked Beanz can. This color has to be the same over all their products and designs, so its color-matching number will be used to ensure there are no differentiations, even when printed in numerous countries worldwide.

Before finally choosing the color, you have to know on which stock you are printing the color, then choose the appropriate swatch book. Choose the color you like and underneath there will be a unique number which you then have to find on screen.

In InDesign, click Windows > Color > Swatches. Go to its dropdown menu and select *New Color Swatch*, where you select the Pantone book you have been using, such as Pantone Solid Matte, then find your color, e.g. Pantone 032 U. Your color will then appear in your swatch.

If your job is for the digital world, it's only screen based and what color you are using is determined by what you see on the screen.

different

The different print proofs and how to check them

Originally for a color litho, a print proof was a wet proof. For this we made the litho plates and pulled a proof from them so everyone—designer, client, and printer—could see what would happen when the exact same printing plates were on press, being printed on exactly the same paper.

Modern technology has made this, like so many other stages in design and print, a thing of the past. At best you get a scatter proof, which is where the color images are all ganged up closer together and then wet proofed.

Cromoline was when the four different films that are used to make the four plates—the C film, M film, Y film, and K film—were laid on top of each other and then exposed together onto a single sheet of photographic paper to show exactly what you would get when the image would be printed on a printing press.

Digital proofs are now the industry norm. The computer information is digitally printed onto paper for you to judge the color; the same digital information is sent to make plates and then forwarded to the actual printing machine to help make ready.

Also on brochures, and essential on books, is a lo-res book proof to show exactly what the final job will look like. This also shows every element is in the correct place and correct order; it is not to judge the color of the pictures. For that you use the high-resolution digital proofs.

High-res digital proofs are essential to check color, type, etc. before you go to press. It gives you and the printing machine minder a visual benchmark to achieve when printing the job.

PDFS are good for checking that all the elements are where they should be but can't be used for checking color, as no two screens show exactly the same tones. In the studio, our computer screens are calibrated to match the main printers' screens, which helps.

Write clearly on all the proofs in red ink what is wrong with them, in similar language to Adobe Photoshop adjustments. Always use plain English and write more, not less, as you are trying to explain in text a visual adjustment. You are trying to get the printer to see that picture the way you are seeing it.

Also check your proofs in the best light standing by a window, as overhead office light tends to yellow most things. If necessary go see the image on the printer's screen so you are both looking at the same thing.

If in any doubt at all after the second proof, attend the press to check printing as it prints.

attend

WEB
SKILLS

EIGHT

The web design game

This section is not a manual or guide on how to design websites, but if your main area of work in your first year is in a web design firm, then knowledge is your key—it informs your design skills.

Because the world of internet design changes and matures at a radical pace, internet design will, by the time this book is printed, have moved on yet again. The rules of this game will have changed.

I believe web design is similar to and moving toward television, albeit an interactive version, because the base, the screen, is essentially the same. Whatever you can do on a big screen you will be able to do on a small screen. We might all end up staring at 3D websites in the comfort of our own homes.

The web will mix the best of book and magazine design with moving images and sound, bringing it into one flawless visual interactive experience.

I view website design as similar to, or as an analogy of, both book and magazine design, where the content is king and the design is there to enhance the content. However diverse this content is, in essence it is purely information design.

If you're a designer, you're into the look and feel of the information, which for a website is the actual layout of the site.

To design to your best advantage, you have to know the limitations of what you can and cannot do in the constantly changing web design world.

The only limitation should be your imagination, not the ability of the developer. If you're a designer, play to this strength and work closely with a gifted programmer who doesn't spend his time telling you

imagination

what you can't do, but whose kick in life is seeing if you can do it.

Printing is a vehicle for disseminating information to the masses, and the web happens to be the new kid on the block to do this. If printing is over five hundred years old, then web design is still pretty much in its infancy.

I can see a time when programs such as InDesign will convert your design into a programmed website where you hit a button and it's uploaded onto the web instead of a print-ready PDF for printers.

> **Form follow fiction.**
> **Find the story.**
> **Know the story.**
> **Distill the story.**
> **Only then should**
> **you make visual**
> **decisions on how to**
> **tell the story. The**
> **best design begins**
> **with story.**
> Leland Maschmeyer

Designing for the web

This chapter might seem out of place in a book about design, but we are not going to be explaining the technicalities of how to code and learn programming. Instead, this is to give you an awareness of what is available and can be incorporated into your concepts and design process.

You don't need to be a coder or a programmer to design for the web; more often than not you'll be doing the visual side and a developer will then build the website. But knowing the media you are working with is always useful and will help you design a more successful website.

You should think of approaching web design in the way you would approach any other type of design: you need to know your target audience, understand the brief, ask the right questions, and know where and how the final product will be viewed and used. Design the solution accordingly.

So should you go out and learn HTML, Java, and PHP if you want to work with web? It's not a requirement, though there is nothing wrong with learning it if you are interested. Knowing more can't hurt.

However, being aware of what is available, what you should consider, and the choices you have will always make you a better designer.

You may also come to a situation where you want to work with a freelance developer to provide a client with a *full-package* product. If you are ever in that position, you will be glad you know how to ask for what you want and that you can communicate with the developer with ease. In fact, being able to communicate with any professionals that also deal with the design industry is something you should learn and be comfortable doing.

How to think in pixels

It can be very daunting to begin designing for web. Somehow the concept of working in pixels can make people hesitant—perhaps it's because these little pixel critters just aren't tangible.

We all grow up with inches and paper sizes—from our first year at school we are wielding rulers almost daily, so it's no wonder how comfortable we are when it comes to thinking in inches to design for print—they are old friends after all.

We know them, what they look like and how big they are. But how big is one pixel?

It's a foreign unit we have little experience with outside of web design, and it takes a while to get used to. But think of it this way: it's just another unit. We all design using type measured in point sizes.

Do you know how big a point is? Or a pica? Probably not. But that doesn't stop you being able to recognize 10-point type as easily as you can recognize 10 inches. Points are a unit created purely for quantifying type and have been used to do so for hundreds of years, despite never being used for measuring anything else outside of typography.

So try not to let the world of pixels scare you. It's just the unit for web design at the moment, just as points are the unit for type.

Familiarize yourself with common pixel dimensions used for the web—different people have different preferences, but most choose to design web pages 900–1,000 pixels wide—and you'll soon be as au fait with pixels as you are with imperial.

Present your folio with passion and enthusiasm. This should be put together in such a way that each project almost speaks for itself! We are talking of visual images here—so powerful and hardly in need of verbal explanation.

A sketchbook is a particularly good idea. This sketchbook can simply contain things that you like. Something you saw in a magazine. A bit of driftwood. Maybe a photograph you took. Any image that excited you and you wanted to capture. Anything—it doesn't matter.

I have to say, as a recruiter for the design industry, I found it was those who had a tidy and well-presented portfolio **plus** a really messy sketchbook containing all sorts of goodies who got the jobs.

Why? Sketchbooks speak volumes about the person and their thought (creative) processes.

Gloria Baldwin

Application of fonts

When the web was in its infancy, the typefaces available and considered web-safe were very limited. Not so nowadays, when the range of typefaces available and optimized for web use is impressively broad; beautiful and interesting typography is no longer restricted to the realms of print. Various web-font hosting services are now available and for a small subscription fee. The web can be your typographic oyster.

But with such abundant choice comes difficult decisions—which typeface should you use and how? First, choose something that is appropriate—both for the content and the platform. Someone once told me they'd seen a gravestone that used Comic Sans; the mind boggles. So read your copy and choose a suitable typeface that is also optimized for web. Also, bear in mind the suitability of a font for the type of copy you are setting; for example, for body copy on the web, typefaces with a larger x-height have the greatest readability values.

Spend time on your typesetting—don't just flow in the copy and stick with the default settings. Reading on screen is a different experience to reading print and you should take this into account. Readability is king, so test your typography by reading it yourself—if you keep losing your place or have to concentrate very hard, chances are the leading needs increasing or the line lengths need shortening. Experiment with different point sizes and leading and compare them: you are aiming for type that is easy to read and digest. A good place to start is having your leading value roughly 140 percent of your text point size—web type needs space to breathe, so don't suffocate it.

Be aware as well that your typography may look different on different platforms, so be sure to test it by viewing it across multiple devices, particularly on differentiate

those that run on Apple software and those that use Microsoft—you may find type that was designed on one looks different displayed on the other.

In terms of browers and display, be aware of updates and restrictions related to type. For example, some browers have recently begun supporting the use of OpenType features such as ligatures and swashes, which could change the look and feel of your typography and achieve a closer resemblance to what you may choose to use for print.

Contrast is a fundamental part of good typography —if your contrast isn't high enough (pale-colored letters on white) then your readability levels will suffer. To test whether you have sufficient contrast, take a screengrab of your website and change it to grayscale in Photoshop.

When it comes to point size, try to resist setting it below 12 points (or 10 points at a push!). Small type on print looks great, but sadly on screen it just can't be read, so bear in mind that a common point size for web type is 16—big enough to be read on both a desktop and a mobile device.

Often, the attention span of people reading on the web is very short—most people scan the page for the information they are looking for. To help them find the bits they want, make sure you have a clear sense of hierarchy in your typography. Make use of italics or small caps or other variations within your typeface's family to differentiate sub headings, links, etc. Follow a clear structure and apply the same treatment to headings and so forth throughout to enable easy navigation for all the scan-readers out there.

Still stuck on which typeface to use? There are lots of recommendations online, from which were the most popular fonts in which year, to the best free typefaces out there (these gems are often hidden among a forest of ugly fonts, so take care when choosing something for nothing). A grasp of good print typography will stand you in good stead for creating good web typography, but paper and pixel are different beasts with different properties and purpose, so treat them accordingly and you should be able to tame both.

flyfishing

Flyfishing and mousetrapping

It is almost impossible to pinpoint the beginning of a creative idea, but there is always that decisive moment when it rises to the surface.

That instant when it changes from a glimmer in the head to a fullblown picture in the mind.

The moment when a phantom thought can be put down as a tangible thing on paper, electronic window, blackboard, shirtcuff, back of an envelope, or notebook.

Unless ideas are nailed down they are likely to vanish. Only when trapped can they be massaged into a reality.

Alan Fletcher, 1994

wire

Wireframing

**Be adaptable;
it's a constantly
shifting landscape.**
Justin Davies

Wireframing is an important initial step in the
production of any design for screen. Wireframes are
to websites what blueprints are to a building: a set of
simple line drawings created at the beginning of the
design process mapping out all the elements, where
they go, how big they are, how they interact with one
another and so on. It is a good idea to start a website
by creating a wireframe as it allows you to focus on
the functionality of the design and the hierarchy of
the information without the distraction of color,
typefaces, imagery, etc. If the basic layout of your
website doesn't work, no amount of beautiful visuals
will help, just as a good wallpaper won't disguise a wall
that is too small or in a funny place. If anything it will
just draw attention to it.

Wireframes are essentially your usability and
functionality checklists, allowing you to decide exactly
what goes on which page and how it works.

The biggest benefit of beginning the design process
by exploring wireframing is that it is much easier and
quicker to change elements around and add things
in a wireframe than it is in a complex, populated
web design; you can save yourself a lot of time.
Wireframes can also help you understand and control
how the user interacts with the site, as multiple
button and navigational behaviors can be represented.

You can begin to create wireframes the old-fashioned
way with a pencil and paper, although some choose to
skip this step. Once you have your sketches, you can
create them in Illustrator or InDesign using a canvas
the correct size for your site and labeled boxes or
shapes to indicate the position and size of each of the
design elements: logo, navigation, footer, etc. At this
stage it is useful to create a base grid to help with the
structure of your site—dividing your page into twelve
equal columns is a good place to start.

Once you are happy with the layout, you can create a grayscale version to help you refine it further, and then a high-definition version by adding the logo and text (still with no color), at which point you can play with typefaces and point size while maintaining the ease of moving things around.

Ideally, when the wireframes are shown to the client, they will request any functionality-based changes they may have, such as adding a wish list function, before the project proceeds to the actual designing of the site. However, be aware that people who aren't designers will sometimes find it difficult to visualize their finished site and how it will work from a wireframe, so don't be surprised if a few sneaky functionality queries are raised later on in the process. Once you do have wireframes that everyone is agreed upon, you can begin to design the site using the wireframes as your guide.

online

SEO and alt tags

SEO or search engine optimization refers to maximizing (or *optimizing*) the ability of a search engine to find your website or images when a specific relevant search is done. When search engines look for websites on a particular topic, they rank the results, ordering them according to what the search engine understands as the most authoritative and relevant results first. So how can you convince a search engine that your site is worthy to be featured, and how can you get higher up in the rankings? The answers lie in SEO.

The relevance of a website to a particular search term is assessed based on the textual content of the site—how many keywords there are and how often they appear. The authoritative value of a site is estimated by the quality and quantity of links that lead to that website—each link from another quality site to yours is like a vote of confidence or endorsement in the eyes of a search engine. Simply put, increasing SEO is based on writing content peppered with the right keywords and building links with other highly regarded sites.

Although SEO is usually a key concern for a developer rather than a designer, it is wise to be aware of it and what it involves as it can inform your design. Perhaps you are designing a site that is largely visual and has very little text—you may want to incorporate text into the design anyway to increase SEO. A beautiful, image-orientated site is all well and good—but not if it is impossible to find in the first place.

One way to incorporate text into a site without featuring actual type on the page is to use ALT tags. An ALT tag or ALT text is the textual alternative to a visual element of a web design—a concise label of what that graphic is and/or the purpose it serves. For example a logo on a website might have the ALT tag of *et al logo*. One purpose of ALT tags is to allow all web users access to the same information, even if they are viewing the content on a text-only device or via a screen reader. In some countries, it is an illegal offence to create websites without proper ALT tags as it can be seen as discrimination to web users who are blind, color blind, or partially sighted.

Another reason to use ALT tags relates back to SEO. It can be helpful when designing a website for you yourself to view the page in a text-only browser, as this effectively replicates how a search engine will view it.

When viewing the textual content of your site in order to rank it, search engines will include the words within your ALT tags; for an image to come up successfully in a Google Image search, for example, it needs to have an accurate ALT tag so that the search engine can find it. Some browsers will also display ALT tags when the cursor hovers over an image, so consider this when writing the tags and make sure they are relevant to the graphic. In cases where the graphic is purely for decoration, and neither represents nor contains information, then an empty ALT tag is preferable to not including one at all, as browsers may revert to reading the file name which is unlikely to suffice as a concise and accurate label.

display

Building with progressive enhancement

Ask questions. Lots of them. Over twenty years as a designer, I have learned the value of collaboration. This starts at your first job and never stops throughout your career.
Not-So-Famous
Brian Collins

Due to the growing number of devices on which the web is viewed, it is increasingly crucial to build online content that is flexible and universally accessible, no matter what gadget is used to view it. One of the nicest things about digital design is its perpetual flexibility; things can always be changed and with instant effect.

One way to create flexible web content is to build sites based on the idea of progressive enhancement. In layman's terms, progressive enhancement is a strategy of web design based on the separation of HTML, CSS, and Javascript; essentially they become individual layers of features—the more features that a particular browser supports, the more features of the full web design will be displayed. And yet on devices at the lower end of the spectrum, the content will still be available, just within a more basic version of the full design. The progressive enhancement design philosophy means that the web experience is enhanced in parallel with the increasing functionality of the user agent, and no consumers are denied access due to the technology they are using.

Building digital content using progressive enhancement is again often the concern of a developer rather than a designer. However, as always, it is helpful to have an understanding of the concept so that it can inform your design process, and also so that you can communicate intelligently and smoothly with said developers.

When designing for the web using progressive enhancement, it's best to begin with the lowest common denominator. Design an HTML site that will work on the broadest possible range of user agents—this is the foundation of your site. Layout and design can be added in the CSS layer, and Javascript is used to add interactive behaviors to create a rich digital experience for those users with devices capable of facilitating it.

By producing web content based around the concept of progressive enhancement, you can be confident that your digital content is accessible to the broadest possible audience, and that while it can still be read by devices such as screen readers, it can also be a rich digital experience to those viewers using the cleverest of devices: essentially, the design tailors itself accordingly.

Responsive web design

It is very difficult to predict how an audience will interact with web content. There are so many different devices they could be using for internet access, and in each category of web platform there are numerous different combinations of features: not all mobile devices will have small screens and touch screens aren't necessarily on small handheld gadgets. And because of the breadth of gadgets available and the number of variables, it is an increasingly gargantuan task to produce versions of a web design for all the different resolutions and screen sizes that the modern audience uses. And yet if we don't optimize our designs for different gadgets, their user friendliness will plummet, and sometimes the design just won't look very good or work very well. Cue responsive web design.

Similarly to the section on progressive enhancement, responsive web design is usually a topic for developers rather than designers. But a basic understanding is good to have.

The concept of responsive web design is about creating design that responds to the device and user behavior and displays the content appropriately, taking into account the screen resolution, platform, and orientation. Think about when a smartphone is used to access the web: we now expect to be able to turn the device from landscape to portrait and vice versa, and for the content on screen to politely adjust itself to accommodate this movement. Prior to design strategies like responsive web design, even this would require the production of two designs if the content were to be equally palatable in both orientations.

Fortunately, by using responsive web design, this process can be streamlined considerably. This design philosophy is based on the use of flexible layouts and grid systems to create web designs that will automatically adjust themselves according to the properties of the device it is displayed on and the behaviors of the user, therefore eliminating the need to produce different designs for the different gadgets or screen resolutions.

It is worth noting that there is a difference between a responsive web design and a fluid web design. A fluid design will adjust itself to fit the size of a browser window; the elements will be organized so that no matter the size of the screen, each feature will take up the same percentage of space.

Fluid web design is a question of maintaining proportions and the aim is to protect the spatial integrity of a design.

However, a responsive site will appear differently—there may be a different number of columns, for example—depending on the device and the user behaviors, not just the size of the screen. Rather than just the one layout being scaled up or down, the layout and features themselves will be tailored to suit that particular device and scenario.

responsive

The power of analytics

One of the most unique and brilliant aspects of the web is that it can be measured. With web analytics, information on web traffic and usage can be measured and reported, allowing us to see how our digital content is used, giving us invaluable insights.

With any piece of print design—such as this book—there is no way to measure the user interaction with it. Yes, we can know how many are sold and where, but what about which pages are read the most? Which are returned to over and over again? Which are hardly read at all? There is no way to tell. But with web, there is.

Web analytics can deliver statistics on the number of people who visit a site, which pages they view, and how many times they view those pages.

This allows you, the designer, to refine or tailor the site accordingly, hopefully increasing effectiveness—and therefore traffic—even further. Web analytics can also help quantify how successful a print or broadcast campaign has been by measuring how much the web traffic has increased by since the campaign's release.

With information on who is visiting a site and which pages they access, research can also be gathered on market trends and consumer behavior, which gives greater understanding of the target audience, thereby allowing them to be targeted even more succinctly in future.

u   nique

Naming web files

Naming files properly is always sensible. You want to be able to locate what you're looking for easily, both during a project and also long after it's all wrapped up—you never know when you might want to dig out a specific file from the past.

Also, there will be times when other people need to be able to navigate your filing system, and if you've hidden things in odd places with odd names, you're probably not going to please them very much.

The same principle applies to naming web files, although as well as making it easy for you to find the files, you're making it easy for a search engine to find them too.

Search engines work by reading the names of files uploaded to a website to get an idea of what the image is—they see an image by reading what it is called.

If you name your files with an irrelevant code that only you can understand, you are shooting yourself in the foot, as search engines will not be able to understand what the file is, and therefore it won't come up when someone looks for it.

You should name your files with keywords that describe what it is.

Stick to one sentence case, either uppercase or lowercase, but not both, and try to keep names to a reasonable length—long file names often result in long URL's, which can deter consumers from clicking on them.

Avoid using underscores to separate words; they confuse matters because they are read as a character rather than punctuation.

Search engines are capable of reading words that run together without any spaces in the same way hashtags are often written.

But if you do wish to use spaces, then hyphens or periods work well, and they make names more legible to human readers, helping to avoid confusion; for example, the name *mensexchange* could mean *mens exchange* or it could mean something very different…

search

How to remove backgrounds from graphics

Give it the overnight test. If it still looks good in the morning, go with it.
James von Leyden

The most prevalent file formats for web graphics are JPEG and GIF—neither of which is ideal for partially transparent images. JPEGs do not support transparency and GIFs (GIF89a files) only support 1-bit transparency. Pixels are either transparent or opaque; they cannot have semi-opaque values, and therefore you cannot achieve any gradual fading effects. GIFs also have a limited palette of 256 colors, which can lower the quality of an image or cause distortion when it is exported in this format.

Because of the limitations of the GIF file format, PNGs were developed.

PNG files are also commonly used for web graphics, and they have the advantage of supporting full and semi-transparency, as well as having a much broader palette of millions of colors.

However, the reason that GIF and JPEG formats remain the most common files for web graphics is that not all browsers support PNG files and their system for transparency, which is based on the use of alpha channels. By using one, you could inadvertently be narrowing your audience simply because their browser will not display your graphics. Tricky.

However, there is a way to cheat. Provided you know against what background your web graphic is going to be displayed, you can change the background of your image to the same color and export it as a JPEG. When it is uploaded, it will have the same appearance as it would have with true transparency. Sneaky, eh?

Of course, if the background of your site is patterned or changes, then flaws begin to appear in this method. But often you will be working against a solid background, so this is a good little get-around in those cases.

173

The pencil is mightier than the mouse.
Martin Ashcroft

It is a common misconception that all images created for web ought to be 72 PPI because computer screens are 72 PPI.

This is a myth, and in truth, the PPI value of web graphics isn't the most important factor—what matters is the width x height resolution. (This is not true of print, where all graphics should ideally be 300 DPI or higher to achieve a professional finish.)

Most digital screens are now 100 PPI or more, and this figure is only likely to increase as we progress into the era of HD. An image with the same width and height pixel values will display the same on a digital screen whether it is 72 PPI, 150 PPI or 300 PPI. The 72 PPI version will be a smaller file size, though, and will therefore be quicker to load, which is why it is the most popular choice for web graphics.

The best way to ensure your graphics appear crisp is to produce the images at the correct width and height to suit the design—it is when graphics are scaled up that the quality is lost. As a basic rule of thumb, create large images at roughly 400–600 pixels wide and 72 PPI, and thumbnails at 100–200 pixels wide and 72 PPI.

You may also want to consider preparing your graphics for HD web—as the pixel density of digital screens continues to increase, we are experiencing the advent of HD web.

The increasing number of devices used to browse the web also means that designs ought to be as fluid as possible, allowing the efficient and successful adaptation of web pages to suit the size and resolution of the screen they are being viewed on. Here are a few simple things you can do to help prepare your web graphics for HD viewing.

Where possible, avoid creating web graphics as bitmap files—aim to use vectors or smart objects in Photoshop as they can be scaled up and down without loss of quality.

Previously, web browsers would only support bitmap images but browsers will now, for the most part, happily support SVG files which are completely scalable. Be sure to check, though, as some browsers will only support certain filters and effects in SVG graphics.

HD or retina screens have double the screen density of a standard digital device; each pixel of an image designed for standard display will take up 2 pixels on a retina screen and therefore the graphic won't appear as crisp, as it is essentially being scaled up to double the size.

One way to conquer this problem is to create two versions for each web graphic, one for standard display and one with double the width and height values for HD display—you can then use Javascript to serve the image that is most appropriate for the device it is being viewed on.

display

Most designers collect all sorts of stuff for reference and inspiration. Many aspire to a minimalist lifestyle—that's a tough combination!
Geoff Haddon

you can't expect to be doing the sexy stuff right off

I could probably talk a lot about how hard it is getting a job, how difficult and demoralising interning can be, etc., but I think there's been a lot said about that already and there's nothing new I can really add. I'd rather share some of my experiences of when I've been in a job—both as intern and as big boy junior designer.

I think one of the things you might need to accept starting out is that you probably won't be doing the work you want to do right away. I don't think I've yet worked on a project I'm particularly proud of, and that might be something to do with the fact that there are a lot more constraints in the real world of work—projects at college were great (while often being unrealistic) in that you can pretty much do your own thing and have complete creative control. It's great to be experimental and creative doing school projects, and you should definitely enjoy what you're doing, but I think a lot of student portfolios don't demonstrate some real world application. Being able to produce work that a client can actually buy is important and is what a lot of employers are looking for in a graduate—I think a lot of students might think it too boring or corporate, but you need to demonstrate that in your folio. But don't stop doing the crazy stuff either. That's the part that might take you to a different level.

I think it's important to work hard with what you are given, but at the same time make sure that you push yourself and be proactive—if there is a brief coming into the agency you aren't working on but want to, then let the right people know you do, or do some work on the side and put it in front of the creative director. Be hungry, but don't be arrogant and expect to be doing the cool work. Any young designer/creative will want (and should want) to be working on the sexy projects, but I think you have to prove yourself first with some of the less glamorous work and make sure you do the best job you can on that. You can't expect to be doing the sexy stuff right off.

Steven Williams

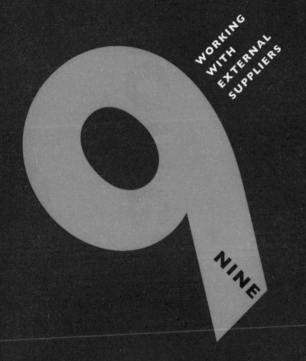

9

WORKING
WITH
EXTERNAL
SUPPLIERS

NINE

illustration

SOLVES

PROBLEMS

How to work with illustrators

Good illustrations help you solve design problems. I always say that if you can't solve the problem alone, get someone who can help or get an illustrator to solve it for you.

Some communication problems are best solved by illustration rather than photography. This is because you can draw concepts that cannot be photographed.

A picture paints a thousand words. The ability to understand when you need an illustration to solve a design job is the beginning of developing your visual toolkit. If the main feeling is that an illustrative solution is needed, do not be tempted to do it yourself; you're a professional designer not a professional illustrator.

Lesson one: if you want a Picasso, don't commission Rubens. Look through all the different illustrators' portfolios for someone who produces the look and feel of what you want.

You will be choosing an illustrator because of their unique ability to illustrate in a certain style and with a certain understanding or approach to their illustration work. You are choosing them specifically because you know their style and ability fits your brief and communicates what you have conceptualized.

Lesson two: let them do what they are good at. Do not over art direct them. Telling an illustrator that you know exactly what you want and how you want it may restrict their creative flow.

If they feel they have handcuffs on, then the final illustration will look like they did it while wearing handcuffs.

Always get a rough to check that the work is solving

the visual problem you want solved. Show the client and get their sign off before the final illustration is done.

If you want a brilliant job in your portfolio, hire a brilliant illustrator and let them run. It only reflects well on you. The best illustrators are the same as the best designers. They are the same breed. Designers solve communication problems by using graphics and illustrators solve the same problem by using illustrations, so work with them and not against them.

Their ideas may be better than yours. If they are, celebrate it, and give them the encouragement and suggestions to achieve the best possible result.

Your design skills and their illustrative skill should form a seamless whole to support the visual message the client wants to communicate

If the design job calls for an illustration, then make the illustration the hero of that piece. A great illustration needs the correct space for it to work and communicate to its fullest. Therefore, always consider how you might be able to bring out the best in the illustration with your considered design and layout.

The key is to guide the illustrator through the brief. Make it clear what the illustration has to communicate and give them a full understanding of what is required (over and above the communication aspect, this may include color restrictions, printing process, and proportions of the final illustration). Stay in constant communication with the illustrator, as the more you communicate, the better it will work.

result

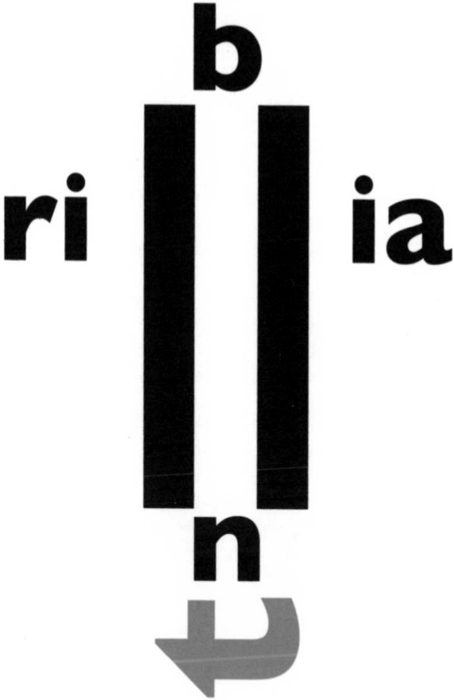
b
ri
ia
n

How to work with photographers

You may think that, as a designer, you can take a great photograph. If that's the case, why are you a graphic designer and not a photographer? It's exceptionally rare that you can do both brilliantly. You are either a photographer or a designer.

To become world class in any discipline, you may need to devote a lifetime to it. You can always come back in the next to do the other!

Working with a professional photographer is very similar to working with a professional illustrator. If you want to use a photographer, you need to work out the look and feel of what you want photographed.

Look at the portfolios of different photographers. They will specialize in certain areas: food photography, fashion photography, still life, interiors, or location work. Look through their work to find the closet piece of their portfolio to the look and feel you want in your work. Work with them to get the best out of the job—art direction can help the final picture, but be careful: the wrong type or too much art direction can put unnecessary restrictions on the photographer.

A good way of explaining the sort of shot you are after is to do a pencil visual of the photograph. This is often the simplest way of explaining your visual ideas to another visual person. Bear in mind that your visual is only going to be a guide.

You should realize that if the communication is resolved by photography, then the photography is the hero, and so it wants to be the predominant aspect of the design. From experience, 50 percent photography and 50 percent design does not work well, as this ratio doesn't do either discipline justice. It needs to be 80–90 percent photography and 10–20 percent design (very often a strong photograph needs very little design to communicate the message).

I If it's a photographic job, then let it be a proper photographic job.

When possible, go to the photography shoot. Don't be afraid to ask to go along and show your willingness to learn. Spending time at the shoot will increase your knowledge base and understanding of the process, showing you how to work effectively within a related field. Always offer an invitation to the client to come along too—this way they can see what they are getting for their money.

A no-no when looking for a photographer is to see a photograph in a top photographer's portfolio or online from a picture library, and then get a cheaper photographer to copy it. This will always end in tears.

Many commercial and advertising images are made up of several images *comped* together, but try to get the photographer to do as much as they can *in camera*. Retouching and post-production are both time-consuming and expensive, often costing even more than the original photography. Photographers use Photoshop with all its possibilities not only to make the image perfect but also to personalize their pictures.

From a photographer's point of view, working with a good designer can be very satisfying because—if they understand each other—two heads can be better than one.

Photographers are craftsmen, not tradesmen.
Julian Calder

How to brief creatives

The more you clearly communicate your idea and the message you want to achieve, the better the result will be. Just like the briefs you get as a designer, they have to convey exactly what you are trying to achieve with this brief.

You are dealing with another creative, so give them as much background detail as possible.

I have, in the past, written down a set of benchmarks I am trying to achieve and given this as a part of the brief. You both now have a common ground by which to judge the final piece. Too tight a brief will not allow this particular person to creatively do what you hired them to do in the first place.

Too loose a written brief means there is room for misunderstandings. They may look at the brief and turn the whole thing upside-down and still produce an amazing result—if so, celebrate it.

You have to believe in the outcome, though, because you are going to have to sell it to your client. And remember, risks are worth taking, beause that is how some amazing work happens.

Without a brief in writing, it is not clear what you are agreeing on. Without it, you can't judge the design work and nor can the client, as neither of you have any common ground to compare it to.

Without an order for creative work in writing, you are potentially doing it for nothing, because nothing was agreed or outlined. No Brief, No Order, No Work.

The difference is that professionals get paid and only amateurs work for nothing. *Unless it's for your portfolio.*

No, Watson, *said Sherlock Holmes,* this was not done by accident, but by design. *Design is what happens between conceiving an idea and fashioning the means to carry it out. Whether big stuff like painting a picture, making a movie, and creating a commercial enterprise or small stuff like rearranging the living room furniture. In short, designing is what goes on in order to arrive at an intelligent equation between purpose and construction, thus converting a problem into an opportunity.*

The British Design Council published fifty definitions of design. The most direct came from a ten-year-old who said, Design is important because if it were not designed it would not be made. *Surprisingly, a few people also earn their living by giving form to the amenities of life, in manufacture, communication, and place. They call themselves designers. They are the blue-collar workers of the art world.*

Whereas painters are concerned with solving their own problems, the designer's role is to solve other people's problems. Actually, that's an oversimplification; the real issue is the elegance of the solution that solves the problem. That is a personal challenge rather than a utilitarian discipline. A commitment rather than an involvement. A difference exemplified by ham and eggs, in which the pig is totally committed whereas the chicken is merely involved.

Designers derive their rewards from inner standards of excellence, from the intrinsic satisfaction of their tasks. They are committed to the task, not the job. To their standards, not their boss. So whereas most people divide their lives between time spent earning money and time spent spending it, designers generally lead a seamless existence in which work and play are synonymous. As Milanese designer Richard Sapper put it:
I never work—all the time.

Alan Fletcher, 2001

JOBS

How to brief and liaise with printers

As soon as you have appointed the printer, having received the print quotations and you and your client are happy to use them, get them in for a briefing to discuss the details of your job. This is a necessary step on the more complex jobs like brochures and small books.

If you think about it, you may be spending weeks to get your best-ever job completed on time. The one thing you do not want is for your best job to be printed badly, so the closer you can work with a printer the better.

Ask them how they want the files, who is going to put the curves on pictures for different stocks, etc. (different paper types require the photographic work to have a different curve applied to them to print to their best on that sort of paper). Ask for their advice; on the whole they will be very responsive. The fact that this job is very important to you means that it has to be perfect.

I have had over thirty-five years of printers' excuses for things not going to plan, and I must say that sometimes it is not their fault. So be clear about the details and ask lots of questions that will clarify exactly what is needed

Some jobs seem jinxed; if they are trouble going through the studio, they will be trouble the whole way, including going through the print process. It just happens. In this case, tell the printer and double-check what is going on at all times throughout the process. If they see how much you care about the job, it also has an effect on their approach to the job.

Like most things in life, you eventually get what you pay for. You won't get the best printing from the cheapest printer.

> **If I had thought it would look better like that then I would have done it in the first place!**
> Karen Billingham

If you add all the design fees, the organization costs, expenses, and the printing costs together, it can be a substantial amount of money. Not to see the job through to the last stage is madness and irresponsible.

If you have never been to a printer, jump at the first chance to go or ask if you can go. The more you understand about the process of printing, the better. Your design, however brilliant, will still look crap if it is printed badly.

The final piece of communication has to have your care and full attention from the concept to holding the finished printed item in your hand.

understand

The value of building these relationships

Building relationships with the people you work with, be it illustrators, photographers, printers, or anyone who can help you achieve what you need for your clients, is like building a new set of good friends.

It is important to build your own team, people you can rely on and trust, those you need when your back is against the wall and you need help to get out of tricky situations you have been put in by your client.

For me it's like having a well-oiled machine, a creative arsenal of the best ammo when I go into battle or playing cards with a hand stacked with aces. It takes a long time to build a great back-up system—it's the same as making friends, and the only difference is that they are business friends.

You have to put effort into forming and building these relationships, because you only get back what you put in.

When you are in trouble, it's your friends that help you get out of it, and I cannot stress how much my network has gotten me out of tricky situations. Some of these guys help you build your creative muscle. Always help them and they will help you. It's great to build respect from other professionals; it rubs off somewhere down the line in your favor.

As a designer you are the general, and these relationships form some heavy-hitting back-up when you are in difficult situations and need it the most.

Like any friendship, the more you get to know them, the more they will get to know you and it makes working together easier.

a corner for the fool

Wit is a serious business. Aristophanes said the brain of the sage has a corner for the fool, Freud related humor to creativity, and Arthur Koestler gave jester equal billing with scientist and artist. In an endeavor to explain this connection, introspective psychologists tend to resort to comical knee slappers like conceptual thinking is a necessary pre-requisite for the experience of humor based on a violation of cognitive expectancies. *An explanation that underlines the fact that trying to define humor is one of the definitions of humor!*

The only sure thing is that humor is rooted in the refusal of circumstances to conform to our expectations. This can be further refined by the music hall axiom that whereas a comic opens funny doors, a comedian opens doors funny. Whereas the first merely tickles the ribs, the second conveys a quick vivid new perception. A sudden switch from one way of looking at something to another. The Polish-Irish-Jewish joke which catches you off balance. Charlie Chaplin eating the sole of his shoe. Being led down the garden path before being yanked into the bushes.

Wit makes connections no one thought of in quite the same way before, exposes a likeness in things that are different, and a difference in things that are alike.

Wit makes sense out of nonsense.

Alan Fletcher

TEN

10

BUSINESS
SKILLS

I read something recently about pricing work—as a recent graduate I always find it awkward pricing work because you almost feel like you haven't yet earned the right to charge a certain amount or that you should be doing it for free because you're young and inexperienced.

It's so easy to undervalue yourself, but, ironically, if you don't value your work, no one else will either! Anyway, the story went like so:

One day Picasso was sitting in a park sketching when a lady walking her dog recognized him as the famous artist. You're Picasso, the artist! she gushed, and she insisted that he draw her likeness there and then. He obliged, taking a sheet of paper and with a couple of quick, simple strokes, he captured the womans profile.

It's perfect! *She exclaimed,* So simple but brilliant!—
How much do I owe you?
Five thousand francs, *Picasso replied.*
The lady spluttered—What?! How can you charge that? It only took you a second!
Madam, *Picasso replied,* it took me all my life.

The moral is that just because you can complete a design job with perceived ease, it does not mean you shouldn't charge a decent amount for it.

You have spent years learning and refining the skills so that things that were once a struggle—and certainly would be for a non-designer—come easily and quickly to you now.

This doesn't mean you can't charge for these skills.

It may look to the client like it's easy for you to do, but you have worked hard to get where you are, and that's worth something.

Alice Belgrove

Basic marketing skills

By getting your first job, and following the first chapters in this book, you will have gained basic marketing skills.

There is no difference in marketing to any other sector in the industry you wish to work in. If you are not marketing to design firms to get a job, your marketing skills are directed at the industry.

You have to go through exactly the same process: research, identifying potential clients, getting through the door, showing your work, writing a proposal, and getting paid.

Enter all design competitions. You need to get noticed in the industry. Success builds on success: if you win awards it not only raises your profile in the design world, but it gives you something to exploit.

Write a blog, and e-mail potential clients, and remember to update your website. Shout about it.

Always ask a client or design company if they will recommend you to another person. Word of mouth, one job leading to another job, is how I have stayed in the game so long.

Nearly all of our work is on recommendation from someone else, so thank you someone, everyone, and please keep doing it.

Never miss an opportunity to tell everyone what you do so well. I always need an incoming flow of interesting communication problems to solve to produce lots of interesting work. It's why I get out of bed every morning.

The money is the by-product of what I do, not why I do it.

I spend my life doing what I love, and doing it all over the world as well as getting paid for it.

What more can you ask for? It's just brilliant fun!

You have to get out and meet people; if you have great work but never leave your studio, you are not going to succeed.

Life does not generally knock on your door. You have to go and knock loudly on life's door: *I want to come in and play, please.*

everyone

Remember that a brief is usually the best expression someone can give you of what they think they want. My experience is that when people get what they want they're usually disappointed. What they really wanted was something they couldn't have imagined and that's why they came to you.
Michael Wolff

The idea of a written proposal is to give the client a clear and simple understanding of the process they are about to undertake. It gives a breakdown of the different stages the work you will be doing for them, a framework to work within.

A proposal is very important, especially for print work, book design, and most creative problem-solving communication. It gives you and everyone else working on the brief a clearer understanding of the amount of work involved. Also, more importantly, it gives your potential client an understanding and explanation of the fees involved.

It is also your selling document: it can get you through the door, introduce you to prospective new clients, land you the contract, and seal the deal.

A rough structure of a proposal is:

1. Cover Page
   This states the project title, who the proposal is prepared for, who has prepared the document, and the date.

2. Contents
   Here you can present a listing of what will be found within the proposal.

3. Our Understanding
   This is where you explain what you understand from what you have been briefed to do. Reiterate what communication problems are to be resolved. It shows you can listen and understand their needs.

4. Familiarization and Analysis
   You can't solve a problem if you're unable to define it. Use this stage to actually state the precise nature of the work, the market, the positioning and all

If someone wants to *play* client, they have to *pay* client.
David Hillman

understand

that you have discovered about their brand and the competition. This can be the larger and more time-consuming part of the process than the actual designing might be.

This phase is where you break down a job into its bare elements and build the information into a form from which you design.

I have been all over the world doing familiarization and analysis. During the process, I need to be able to feel a job, smell it, touch it, and understand local culture. I also want to have an understanding of how the target audience will perceive things.

All of this gives me a sixth sense of what I am dealing with. Only then do I go for the jugular.

Any large problem can be broken down into a series of smaller, easier-to-solve problems. Just like any large word is explained by lots of small ones.

When you are starting out in the design world, you won't naturally get involved in this phase of the job. You will get the result to ponder over in the design brief. If and when you get the opportunity to be involved in this stage of the work, jump at it. The more you understand the enemy, the easier it gets to win the war.

You are in the game of communication, so you have to learn the client's language, the way they talk and see the world. The more you understand them and what they want to communicate, the easier it is for you to visualize that communication into your own design language.

This whole phase, in its entirety, can end up with large written reports and presentations, culminating in the brand propositioning and a set of benchmark

define

input

qualities by which the clients and designers can judge the creative output.

I have thrown design briefs back at the business analysis people if the brief is not clear or missing what is needed to design with, much to the analysis people's amazement, as they think *he is only a designer, he doesn't understand this.* It's not rocket science.

If they haven't defined the problem and articulated it clearly enough, you won't be able to answer it with graphic design.

If they want the design concept stages very diverse, then it means they haven't done their job properly. Take them on, don't back down, don't give an inch, don't shoot until you see the whites of their eyes. You will lose the war if this stage isn't focused enough.

You can see from the amount of text here how important this phase is in ensuring good communication and great design. It is where the concepts live, like seeds under the ground, waiting for your creativity to bring them to life.

5. Design Concepts
   This is the phase where you come up with great ideas. I present this phase in black and white, very rough. If an idea is strong in simple black and white, it can only be enhanced by color. I need the client to become part of the design team and to understand what we are getting at with this series of ideas.

   This stage is normally carried out in the design studio, and from it around three or four ideas are worked up ready to present to the client. I believe clients are creative, and I want their input into the work. In these meetings it is up to us as designers to be able to communicate the full extent of the information about the client and the possible solutions.

design

Understanding how the client thinks, and creating the dialogue from there, helps us to understand their needs better. No one can communicate what they are trying to do through visuals alone, so meetings can be hugely productive times. Clients say important things in the meetings that need to be visualized there and then. I have been known to draw the logo in front of their eyes. It is magic to a client, but beware, it doesn't always work—this is not a game you play unless you are highly skilled with a hell of a lot of experience and confidence.

6. Design Concept Finalization
   From the first design phase concepts, you come out of the client meeting with hopefully three routes to go away with and develop into more considered and finalized ideas in color. You never see a logo in isolation; it is always implemented, so always show the logo working in context on something like a business card and a homepage. The meeting at the end of this stage is to finalize which route to take forward.

7. Design Development
   This is what I call destruction testing; apply the design route to a selected range of marketing collateral: stationery, signage, banners, advertising, websites, and merchandising products. Also demonstrate interaction with other media.

8. Artwork
   This stage is to produce all base elements and finalize the characteristics of the design identity and its agreed applications. Also produce digital files and specifications for master artworks.

9. Brand Guidelines
   Use all the design elements in the development to explain the essence of the brand. Examples of these elements show how the brand can be used.

explain

10. Communication
    Tell everyone internally within the corporate company, for whom you've just created the brand, what is going on before the design is launched externally.

11. Fees and Costs
    Having worked out what is involved, put the number of days each phase will take to complete and multiply it by your daily rate and you will have the cost. As a rule of thumb, I use between 10 and 20 percent of the fee to cover normal studio costs such as laser printers, color runouts, portfolios, foam boards, etc.

12. Terms of Business

13. Your Résumé

14. Terms and Conditions

15. Schedule of Timings Calendar

    Write a schedule with dates for each stage in the job. This gives you your deadlines and also meeting dates for your client's diary. More importantly, never miss a deadline.

16. Sign Off
    This sheet forms a contractual agreement that what is contained within the proposal is agreed upon. It is for both you and your clients to sign off with a signature.

    Good luck!
    Don't forget to design the proposal brilliantly as it demonstrates what you are going to be doing for them.

Invoicing

What a joyous situation to be in! You are getting paid for what you love doing. Depending on your Terms of Business in your proposal, you will have decided your terms of payment.

I invoice each stage of the job upfront, and never start the next stage unless I have received payment for the previous stage. I like to get a client used to paying me like this, as it focuses his mind on the job, and I hope they will keep this good practice up.

It is sometimes tricky to get the client to pay before you start work, but I explain it by saying to the client that you have agreed to do the job and that their cash flow is better than yours.

If they are committed to the job, they are going to pay at some point so why not now? This normally works.

Your invoice should be a beautifully designed piece of typography just like everything else you do. It references the proposal and the quotes you gave, which have been agreed in writing in the contract (that clearly explains what you have done). List all outside costs, stage by stage.

Never invoice for more than you have quoted in your proposal, unless you have already got that in writing and their approval. Match your invoice to quotations, and then there will be no argument or excuses not to pay.

Always put in writing the changes or extras relating to fees before undertaking the work, however busy you are.

I have a rule: even if I am up against some insane deadline, I stop everything to write the invoices each month. It is the only way to stay in business. Cash

Always build trust and honesty with your clients. Never make them feel they have been overcharged and always be clear on charges before your project commences. Word of mouth is a great marketing tool.
Clayton Lloyd

flow, money going out before it comes in can cripple a small organization very fast.

My invoice is basically the same design as my letterhead with full legal requirments, but with all the bank details and tax details added on it.

I have for years started this small print by saying that if you have any problems with this invoice apart from the cost, please contact me, and then I put in my office details.

I even try to get the accountant to smile.

i didn't sign a contract...mistake

In my first year after graduation, a friend of mine who works in a creative agency approached me to pitch an illustrated idea to a well-known fashion brand. I was excited and spent a few days working up my initial illustrations before submitting them to my friend, for which I was paid a small, fixed free.

This was the first time I had worked on a project like this and I trusted the agency to take care of the work I provided so I didn't sign a contract...mistake.

A few weeks later, my friend told me that the work was very well received by the fashion brand who wanted to roll out my designs across Europe...YAY!

How exciting!

However, I heard no more about when they wanted the finished artwork produced by or any other details, only to find out some weeks later that the fashion brand had taken the concept and illustrations that I had pitched and used another artist to copy them, completely ripping off my designs and using them regardless.

I was very disappointed and, after a few apologetic e-mails with my friend, accepted some money and products from the company, but this paled in comparison to what I had really wanted: the experience of working with them and the final piece for my portfolio.

Never trust anyone else to protect your work; there are plenty of people out there who will happily take advantage if you don't know your rights and exercise them. Just because a brand has big feet, it doesn't mean you should let them stand on you.

No Name
One does not throw stones in a glass house, and the design bussiness is a very fickle thing, but be streetwise.

The correct e-mail etiquette

On the whole e-mail has now taken over from letters. I receive a phenomenal amount per day. They are not as nice to receive as a letter printed on a nice cotton paper with a great design on it.

The main point to remember when composing your e-mail is the fact that you are a designer and everything you touch or do should reflect that. You have a number of choices to make about font, text size, etc.

I find even designers who send me e-mails just keep writing and writing and you end up with very long lines that are very hard to read. If a line of type is too long, it's hard for the eye to get back to the beginning of the next line, so try to keep the line length to a maximum of ten words. You can bring your dialogue box into a smaller measure, but that is asking the recipient to do something or it's left to chance.

You are a designer who works with type every day, so lay out the e-mail the way you want the recipient to see it and have some fun.

Alan Fletcher, while still at Pentagram, would not allow his secretary to send a letter out that had any form of correction on it, no Wite-Out, no self-correcting on the IBM, etc. This did drive some secretaries mad as they typed the same letter for the eightieth time trying to avoid a mistake. But everything going out was perfect, and clients began to notice this over time. It said a lot about the designer they hired.

Your sign-off is also important. It contains your address details (and in our case, all legal corporate requirements), but it can also be used to highlight your client's visual identity and events that may be coming up for them.

File all correspondence

Keeping all work files, be it on your computer, the server, or in folders with printed hardcopies. I still prefer a printed hard copy in a folder, labeled with the client's name. I can pick it up and see the whole history of the job and all correspondence in one go. I do not find it so easy to be constantly opening and closing files on a computer.

The best bit of advice I heard (which I still can't get right) is to only touch the correspondence once, then either file it or bin it.

You will never end up with piles of paper everywhere, as I still do. If everything is filed away, any member of the design team can pick it up and understand what is going on. Ask the correct person for the studio you are in.

I have a rule, which I have spent my life trying to get implemented. Nothing should go to a client without a hard copy in that file.

If a client rings up, or another member of the design team wants to see something fast because the client is on the phone, then it is always on hand.

It is a basic business skill to develop your own list of design companies with your research on them, letters written, and their responses. It is the same for filing your marketing as it goes through exactly the same stages.

> **Carved into a piece of stone were the immortal words: MISTAKES ARE YOVR BEST IDEAS.**
> Dr Phil Shaw

You have been doing this since you put your final year show up or trying to get internships before finishing your degree (see page 28).

What you are selling is your ability to create the sort of work in your portfolio.

Actually, it is about being given the opportunity to create that next, even better design piece you know you can do, if only you get the opportunity to do it and prove you can. So it will lead to the next and the next.

I am still doing exactly the same now as I did when I took my portfolio around London after completing my course.

I just want the chance to create, solve problems, play, and have fun. If you don't have passion for what you do, no one else will. Passion and craft is infectious.

Your passion and belief in what you create will sell your ideas ; as long as you have answered the brief the client is going to be ready to go along with you.

How you feel about the work, from the way you describe the solution to your enthusiasm and passion, will help sell the concept. If you do not believe in the solution or think it isn't good, it will be very hard to convince anyone else that it is.

Having been pushed into a corner by a demanding client to do exactly what they want, one of my last lines of defence to say to back to them is, *If I had designed this like this, you would not have hired me in the first place.*

I have turned down a lot of design jobs that I felt were not going to work because of the client's attitude and

e
s
e

the knowledge that I would not be able to change it.
There is no point fighting to change something, which,
by its very nature, is impossible to do.

It has been said about me by a very powerful director,
Why do we need to hire Cleaver, he always argues with
me. Can't we get a designer who just does what we tell
him to? No, said another director, that is why he is
so good; we don't want a yes man. We want someone
who will take us on, take us out of our comfort zone and
resolve this communication problem, once and for all.

I was once sent a book as a thank you from a client
and the dedication read, *For the designer who always*
asks why.

Once, in a briefing, I was asked by a housing
organization to produce my concept ideas for free.
The other design company had agreed to do the same,
so the organization could judge which company to give
the whole fee to.

I explained that if the other design company did not
know what they were doing that was their problem,
not mine, and I told them I didn't need the practice.
I got the job, there and then, based on my attitude.

yourself

Dealing with clients

It has been said that design without clients would be an ideal world. But without clients, we do not have a design problem to solve.

If you self-initiate your work, you are a fine artist, not a commercial artist or designer. I love clients; they are what make design such a never-ending game. It takes two to tango, so make the most out of each client and situation you are in. I like interesting clients with communication problems that say, *You can't do this can you?* or *There is no way to solve this problem.* Then, I am drooling.

We are, after all, a service industry, and our job is to be of service to the client, so treat clients with the respect they deserve. If you go through life treating everyone the way you like to be treated, you can't go far wrong.

Keep the clients up to date on the work, especially where there might be any problems, like scheduling or budget requirements. If they are late supplying something for you to work with, gently remind them. If it gets too late, warn them in advance of how long printing will take and that you need *x* information by *y* date in order to meet the deadline. It helps place the process more in context for them. Explain that if you do not have the content then you can't meet their schedule.

Work with them; help them achieve what they need to do and be ready to offer alternative solutions in time-critical situations. Explain clearly if what they want is realistic within the time scale they have allowed.

Always be polite and explain to people who are non-designers in a clear manner, just like you would to your parents. You live in a visual world and speak

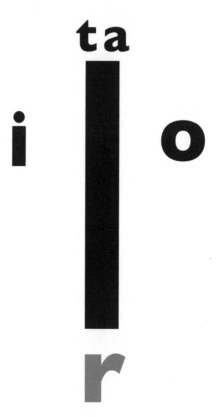

a visual language, they do not. They might not understand what you visually take for granted.

In addition, they might not be able to spot the visual subtleties of a design option, for example, a type-style change or tweak of size. Help them to see the refined details that make the design work. It is about continual communication as well as about managing their expectations.

Make the whole experience like going to the world's best tailor: everything is tailor-made to suit that client, handstitched, beautifully crafted, and fits like a glove with no awkward pulls, making the wearer feel extra special. Develop your natural intuition and learn to be one step in front of them, anticipating their every need.

The more respect and help you provide a client with, the better they will treat you. Don't forget that this relationship is what will lead to your next job, and the next job will be the best you have ever done.

As a junior designer, you can practice on the creative director or the designer who is leading that job. They are your clients at this early stage of your career, so practice it over and over again in your design crits and team meetings.

Join in with the studio, work hard, and always ask before you leave in the evening whether there is anything you can do to help, especially if someone is having to work late to meet a deadline.

Anticipation and awareness are key, not just in your relationship with the client but also in the studio.

Always offer to make tea and coffee before you are asked to. Try to help the jobs run smoothly for the designer above you, and ask if you can help out by saying something like, *Should I call the supplier, will we need more mounting board for that presentation?* Be proactive. If you do only what you're asked to do like an obedient servant, but don't engage the brain to see the whole procedure beyond, you will not make yourself irreplaceable.

You want them to think, *What I am going to do when they leave, they are like my right hand, I don't want to lose this one, they make my whole life easier.* So stay engaged, show that you are willing, and be prepared to work hard. If you put in that extra bit of groundwork early on, you are more likely to be successful later on down the line.

And by the way, whatever you do, don't have an affair with someone in the studio. It only leads to trouble. As my old mum used to say, *Don't shit where you eat.* If you fall in love, change jobs. It is much simpler in the long run.

Another very appropriate age-old saying, *Don't mix business with pleasure.* There's a lot of common sense and truth in this; of all designers I've known who have had affairs with their young associates, none of the young associates have stayed working in that design company for very long. Affairs happen, but be aware of the possible knock on effect to your career.

ELEVEN

END
MATTER

ter min

o o

boy

Y

Terminology and definitions

Aliasing: when the edges of a text or image have hard-pixel edges. See anti-aliasing.

Anti-aliasing: when the edges of a text or image have been smoothed so the edges appear to blend in.

Artwork: a general term for everything from illustrations and paintings to photographs.

Bad break: refers to widows or orphans or any break that causes text to break weirdly or look awkward.

Bandwidth: the rate of data transfer. Usually measured in bits per second (bps).

Baseline: an imaginary line which letters sit on.

Batch processing: the method of quickly changing a lot of information at the same time. See page 119 for how to do this in InDesign.

Bitmap: any image made of pixels (independent of format).

Bleed: when an item, photograph, or color goes over the trim-line.

Cascade Style Sheets/css: language used to describe the presentation of a web page, i.e., the look, formatting, font size, and type, etc. It means if you want to change the appearance of a particular element on the page, you only have to do so once on the css.

CMYK: name of the four-color printing methods. Stands for Cyan, Magenta, Yellow, and Black.

Color bars: used to check the right amount of ink is going into the paper. They are printed just off the edge of the page and have the percentage of each color in them.

Color Matching System: different systems used to ensure color accuracy between the different people involved in a project (e.g., the printers and the designer). See page 79.

Compression: a way of reducing file sizes.

Concept: the idea that will carry the design.

Copy: the text supplied.

Coverage: the area of print.

Cracking: where the paper splits and the ink cracks, normally along a fold. See litho-score.

When I first started working as a designer I would show my mom my jobs. She always said the same thing, *That's nice dear.* And then she'd ask if I did the drawing or took the photograph or wrote the words, and I'd say no. Then I realized and I explained. Before I started there wasn't anything, I made it happen. It's called design.

Brian Webb

Crop/trim marks: lines off the printed area to guide where to trim the documents.

Deadline: the latest date and time by which you must get your work done. Also defined as the only rule in design.

Dot spread/gain: the ink spread from a single dot when it hits the paper.

DPI: specifies the resolution of an output device or file. Stands for dots per inch.

Dummy: a sample of the print job, using the stock that will be used for the final proof.

EPS: a format that can hold vector and bitmap information at once. Stands for Encapsulated PostScript.

Etiquette: the appropriate code of conduct and polite behavior within society or wherever you have the pleasure of working.

Export: when a file is saved in a format intended for another program

Extenders: the parts of the letter that go above the x-height, e.g., on the letter *b*.

Exworks: it means it will be delivered but it's not known where, so the printers have not added delivery to their cost estimate.

File format: the file type indicates how the data is stored. Some are produced by specific software, e.g., .psd files are produced using Adobe Photoshop. See pages 96, 126, and 173.

Finishing: anything that happens to your work after it has gone through the printing press.

Foam board: a strong yet lightweight material that is used to mount photography or portfolio work.

gsm: unit of weight measurement for paper, stands for grams per square meter.

Gutter: the width between columns or the white space formed by the inner margins of the spread near the spine.

Glyph: a single written symbol bearing a non-verbal piece of information.

Hard copy: the physical printed version of a design.

After art school, figuring out who to work for was far harder than finding my way to class. Where was Google in 1991?
Not-So-Famous Brian Collins.

figuring

HTML: the main language used to create web pages.

Imposition: the process of arranging pages on the press so when printed and folded they fall in the correct order.

Hyphenation: a punctuation mark that divides or combines words or syllables, especially when split by the end of a line.

Interface: visual indicators that allow a user to interact with an electronic device, website, or software. Basically how a website, operating system, or program looks.

Justified: (also called fully justified) is where a column of text is aligned on both the right and left.

Kerning: the horizontal space between letters.

Key-line: lines used as a guide over finished work to show the position, shape, and size of other elements that will appear in the layout.

Language: it refers to a way to communicate instructions to a computer. In the context of design it is typically used to create software, websites, and other electronic interfaces. Examples include HTML, XHTML, PHP, Java, and C, among others.

Leading: vertical space between lines of text.

Ligature: a typographic character combining two or more other characters. See page 125.

Linotype: first major mechanical system to cast a solid line of character, now produces Linotype for digital designs.

Literal: wrong character in setting type or printing.

Litho-score: a printing method that creates a heavy impression to create a sharp fold on heavy paper.

Logotype: a single piece of typography that is specifically providing a client's visual identity.

Lossy: a way to compress data in a file.

Margins: invisible guidelines delineating a page.

Master page: a template which can be set up and used as a template throughout a whole document.

Measure: the width of the column of text.

Microns: unit of measure for the thickness of heavy papers and boards.

true

Mock-up: an example of how a design is going to look. Normally used to gain feedback from users or clients.

Monotype: major mechanical typesetting system, used to cast individual characters.

Mounting: the process of displaying work with a strong back to a professional finish.

Optimization: cuts down the file size while trying to maintain its appearance.

Orphan: when the first line of a paragraph appears on its own at the bottom or top of a page or column. See bad break.

Overprint: to print on a printed area.

Pagination: the number of pages and their order.

Pantone Matching System: a system used to ensure accurate color. See pages 80 and 145.

Pixelated: when you can see the pixels that make up an image or type.

Pixels: an area of illuminated space on a screen, miniature in size and by which an image is composed.

Plant list: a list of the machinery a printer has.

Platform: the basic framework of a computer's software and hardware. Its platform defines how it operates and which software it can use.

PP: printed page. Sometimes you'll see 2pp meaning a document has two sides both of which are printed.

Point: or pt, unit to measure type size and spacing.

Post-rationalization: the method of giving meaning to an already created piece of work.

Proof: a copy shown as a close replica to the final printed material.

Raster: a dot-matrix structure used to display graphics. Resolution dependent, meaning it will lose quality when re-sized.

Registration (marks): usually represented by a circle with a cross through it. Helps the printer correctly align the colors. See page 133 for more print marks.

Résumé: an account of an individual's professional history and qualifications. See page 15.

RGB: name of three color method used for web. It stands for Red, Green, Black.

**Nothing more or
less, every advice
is a golden key!**
Doris Chan

advice

Shiner: a percentage of a color (typically Cyan is used) printed under another color (typically Black) to make it richer.

Shingling: an allowance made during prepress to compensate for creep, normally used to compensate for the alignment of page numbers.

Signage: the collections of signs that are used particularly for commercial or public use.

Sign-off: where something is approved by either the client or your art director simply by applying their signature.

Silk/satin art: art paper with a very, very light finish but not quite as glossy as gloss art paper.

Sit up: expression used to describe the way in which the ink sits on the paper, e.g., coated paper will help the ink sit up.

Spot color/special color: a specific or specially mixed color.

Sprite: a collection of images on a web page that can be moved or changed as one graphic.

Stock: the paper that a printer has available in store.

Swatch: samples, often of fabric color.

Typesetting: the process of arranging and composing written material ready for printing.

Wireframe: a visual guide defining the very basic framework of a website. They are used to arrange the various elements that need to be incorporated into a page.

This book contains quotes from some of the most eminent and influential designers of the 20th century. You'll probably not have heard of some of them, but it is your duty as designers to know the history of your own profession and the people who broke the ground that you now tread, so find out who they are.

Acknowledgments

Like the game I compare the design world to, I may be the most well-known player, but I could not win games and the design wars without a team. As with most of my design life, I work in teams, albeit now as the creative director—or whatever title the studio gives me (some of the titles are not as polite). In my role as creative director, I am the driving force behind the work.

Having grown some studios into quite large concerns in the past, I now keep it very small—I want to be actually designing the majority of my time, which I now do, but this work would never have come out without the great help I received from my team.

Special thanks must go to Rosanna Bianchini who does the majority of translating *Phil scribble* into some form of readable and understandable English and telling me when things do not work. Her invaluable assisantance over twenty-eight years of unflinching dedicated sevice, often in the face of very stubben resistance, is deeply appreciated. Why is she always right?

I couldn't have done this without Emma Fisher and Jenny Penny in my studio, with their never-ending paitence and their invaluable assistance on my numerous design adventures.

To Karen Billingham, who has worked with me over the last twenty-five years—the best mark-maker and right-hand you could possibly ever have. Phil Evans, a brilliant designer, for being my perfect foil and strategic genius whose Welsh blood is pure design.

To Alice Belgrove, whose encouragement and supply of many quotes and stories from her young designer friends, alongside her ability to translate most of the web text into very understandable nuggets, I am forever indebted.

Perfection is not just a word—it is a description of this invaluable guide into the byzantine world of design, and how to navigate through it successfully.
Jan Stael von Holstein

audience

To Emily Fairbank, who has worked very closely with me, with a lot of laughter, as one dyslexic to another —or as I kept saying, *The blind leading the blind will work*, nothing stops me. It can and did work. Having dyslexia is like having a super power, in my case helping me see things differently.

Sophia Kossoski, who as an intern was thrown in the deep end on this and has swum like a swan, feet paddling like crazy underwater, calm and serene on top. Martin Ashcroft, our next intern, hit the ground running and had to keep running in the sprint to the finish, his input was great.

Zara Larcombe from Ilex, with whom over lunch at my club, the Savile, this adventure first took route and started me on this path.

Nick Jones also of Ilex for sorting out the word polishing; it was very dirty. To my editor, Jennifer Eiss, for having the courage to leave most of the text alone so it still sounds like me while making it understandable to a greater audience. I am forever greatly in her dedt.

For Raffaell Fletcher for providing Alan's quotes. How could I go to press without them?

To the man that changed the face of British illustration, Brian Grimwood, for his drawing of me, drawn live in a lecture he gave at School of Art and Design at Middlesex University, London.

Finally, to all my well known and respected design heroes, alongside the very young designers who have contributed quotes to make this book what it is.

You are all named with very, very **great pride**.

> If I create from
> the heart, nearly
> everything works;
> if from the head,
> almost nothing.
> Marc Chagall
> I know no other
> way to design.

Who is this guy?

Perhaps the most important consideration when commissioning graphic design is to expect the designer to solve the problem with grace and style.

If, on the other hand, you also get an idea with some new thinking, executed to sublime perfection on time and on budget, you know you asked the right person.

...I have just described Prof. Phil Cleaver.

David Holmes. September 2013

> Phil came to share
> his experience
> with our design
> students in
> Vietnam and
> from start to end
> commanded the
> room. Not one to
> mix words, he's the
> kind of inspiration
> every student
> looks for.
> Richard
> Streitmatter-Tran,

Index

There is no index, sorry. Since this book is written and designed by a designer, I thought it was better not to have one. Most designers naturally do not go anywhere near index pages.

The contents page explains where everything in the book is, and if you can't see what you're looking for in the list of contents, then sadly, I have not written the answer you seek.

If you are sitting in a studio, stuck, your best option now is to Google it, or phone a friend. If all else fails, keep the design faith, life will get better in the end.

DON'T EVER FORGET

R. H. Macy failed four times with retail ventures before his store in New York caught on.

John Creasey failed a lot, he got 743 rejection slips before he published nearly 600 books under twenty-eight different pen names.

You might fail initially, but don't give up trying whatever age you may be, as in the end you can win. Milkshake-mixer salesman Ray Kroc was fifty-two before he launched the McDonald's empire. Colonel Harland Sanders launched KFC after receiving his first retirement check.

Don't worry about failing. You couldn't walk the first time you tried. It took a few goes to learn how to ride a bike. You couldn't swim the first time you went in the water. You shouldn't be scared of failing; you should be scared of the opportunities you'll miss if you never try.

Prof. Phil is a multi-award winning designer, who sees things differently. Protégé of Anthony Froshaug, Phil honed his design and typographic skills under Alan Fletcher at Pentagram in 1977, Wim Crouwel at TD in Holland, and Michael Wolff at Wolff Olins. In 1984 Allied International designers recruited Phil as creative director of branding. In 1987 he established CleaverLandor, a specialist design consultancy. ¶ Since setting up *et al design consultants* in 1992 Phil has been the creative driving force behind a wide range of large brand/corporate identities, pan-European packaging and a phenomenal number of award-winning book designs.¶ Phil is a fellow of the Chartered Society of Designers, a founding trustee of The Monotype Type Museum, a board member of the International Type Academy, and a Fellow of the Royal Society of Arts. Artistic director to The Type Archive.¶ Alongside running *et al* and t.r.u. [Typragraphic Research Unit] he is Professor in the Creative Industries in the School of Art and Design at Middlesex University, London.¶ His reputation is such that his early typographical work is archived in St Bride's Printing Library and his book design is in the permanent collection of the Victoria and Albert Museum's National Art Library.